Bob Izumi's
101 Best
Fishing Tips

DATE DUE

Bob Izumi's 101 Best Fishing Tips

By Bob Izumi

With a Foreword by Craig Ritchie

FIREFLY BOOKS

A FIREFLY BOOK

Published by Firefly Books (U.S.) Inc. 2001

First Printing

U.S. Cataloging-in-Publication Data
   (Library of Congress Standards)

Izumi, Bob.
   Bob Izumi's 101 best fishing tips / Bob Izumi. –1st ed.
[160] p. : col. ill. ; cm.
Includes index.
Summary : Television show fishing expert's best tips on sport fishing.
ISBN 1-55209-560-6
1. Fishing. I. Title.
799.1 21   2001   CIP

Published in the United States in 2001 by
Firefly Books (U.S.) Inc.
P.O. Box 1338, Ellicott Station
Buffalo, New York, USA
14205

www.fireflybooks.com

Published in Canada in 2000 by Key Porter Books Limited

Electronic formatting: Jean Lightfoot Peters
Design: Patricia Cavazinni

Printed and bound in Spain

Contents

Foreword

As I peer out the truck window into the semidarkness, my eyes slowly come to focus on Bob Izumi as he trudges across the parking lot. Ah. We're not home yet, we've only stopped for coffee.

Half a dozen bikers watch Bob as he picks his way across the pavement. Leather-clad, tattooed, bearded, and pierced, they walk as a group, intent on intercepting him before he disappears inside. At one time I would have been concerned, maybe even afraid that he was about to be mugged. But now, I know that all they want is Bob's autograph and some fishing advice.

Fast-forward about six months. We're driving in a light snow, trying to find a parking spot before we head into a spring fishing show. I glance at my watch as we park our vehicle. Bob is expected at a particular booth in an hour and a half. Although this booth is just four or five aisles from the entrance of the center, I know we'll never make it on time. We slip in through the entrance, take half a dozen steps inside and a young boy points, "Look! It's Bob!" Immediately, Bob is surrounded. An hour and a half later, he's only halfway to the appointed booth. Everyone wants an autograph, everyone wants to say hi. And every introduction concludes the same way, "Bob, can you give me any tips?"

That, my friend, is why you're holding this book.

My introduction to Bob Izumi came when I was working as a freelance writer more than 10 years ago. At that time, I inherited the job of overseeing an "Ask Bob Izumi" advice column appearing in *Outdoor Canada* magazine. The job was simple enough—first forward reader mail to Bob for reply, then select some of the better letters and responses for publication. Some people wanted advice on products; other people wanted Bob's opinion on the best lures; still others wanted to know about good fishing locations. Everyone wanted some sort of fishing tip.

That so many people turn to Bob for fishing advice is no surprise at all. His *Real Fishing Show* has been the most popular television fishing program in Canada for 17 years. It's now syndicated coast-to-coast and across the northern United States. In fact, the show now airs worldwide, with viewers from as far away as Thailand and mainland China. Bob's been profiled in virtually every major fishing magazine, as well as most daily newspapers.

Proving that he can do more than just talk a good game, Bob is also by far one of the most successful professional-level tournament anglers in North America, with dozens of first-place finishes to his credit. Since 1974, when Bob's father, the late Joe Izumi, organized the first Canadian bass tournament on southern Ontario's Rondeau Bay, Bob has dominated competitive fishing in Canada. No one else has been able to match his record of consistent top 10 finishes, Angler-of-the-Year titles, and Pro Bass Classic appearances.

Yet unlike many professional tournament anglers, Bob is not just a one-species wonder. He does it all. Bass in Ontario and Quebec. Salmon in British Columbia and Nova Scotia. Pike in Manitoba and Saskatchewan. Lake trout in Quebec and the Northwest Territories. Stripers in Arkansas. Tarpon in Florida. He fishes for walleye, brook trout, steelhead, muskie, panfish, and saltwater species too. Bob's travels have taken him and his fishing gear around the globe, including jaunts to Australia, Cuba, Mexico, Tasmania, and the most remote reaches of northeastern Siberia. He's fished with many of the world's best anglers, top guides, and favorite celebrities. Yet he can still have fun catching sunfish in a local pond with his kids.

Bob's rise to the top began in the early 1980s when he quit his factory job and, with a $10,000 bank loan, gambled on a career as a full-time, professional fisherman. His abilities with rod and reel, combined with his work ethic and friendly nature, have resulted in an angling empire. In partnership with his brother Wayne, Bob has taken his television and radio shows to every major market in the country, launched his own magazine and, more recently, a busy website, making Real Fishing a truly multimedia entity. Fishing lures, fishing rods, fishing boats, and even fishing shoes bearing Bob Izumi's signature fly off the shelves as quickly as the manufacturers can supply them.

Who better to ask for some cool fishing tips?

The title of this book is probably somewhat misleading. This book does far more than simply present 101 great tips from one of North America's top anglers. It takes you on a journey as Bob relives some great fishing moments, many of which have never been revealed before. You will see sides of Bob that the television camera simply can't begin to capture, and you'll travel back in time to understand how he developed so many of the fishing concepts we take for granted today. By the end of the book, you will have shared many of the experiences that have made Bob Izumi one of the world's best-known fishermen. You can't help but come away a much better angler.

If you have a budding interest in fishing, do yourself a favor and read this book from cover to cover. You'll learn a huge amount and have many laughs besides.

If you are a fairly serious angler already, you will find numerous tips throughout this book that will make your time on the water more productive. Plus, you'll enjoy the stories.

If you are a die-hard, phone-in-sick-because-the-salmon-are-running type of angler, the kind of person who periodically leaves work early due to questionable last-minute appointments with some mysterious Dr. Pike, then read this book as soon as possible. You don't want your buddies to read it first, do you?

Perhaps fishing is not the most important thing in life. But have you ever heard anyone on their deathbed complain that they didn't devote enough time to working? Me neither. Life is short. Fish hard.

Craig Ritchie
Editor, *Real Fishing Magazine*

CHAPTER 1

Basic Fishing Tips

Basic Fish Needs

Tip 1

There really are few absolutes in fishing. But the one thing that never seems to change, whether you're fishing for bass in Tennessee or trout in Nova Scotia, is that all fish have basic needs. And, if you understand these needs, locating fish becomes much easier. These needs are food, shelter, and comfort.

Once, while fishing in British Columbia, my guides and I encountered a superb example of food influencing fish location. We were fortunate to discover a small section of the ocean that boiled with tiny, hatching shrimp. Well, it wasn't long before a huge school of herring found these tasty shrimp. And who do you suspect was hot on the heels of the herring? You guessed it—a pack of chinook salmon.

On another occasion, while taping a segment for the *Real Fishing Show* with veteran fishing guide Hugh Albright, we were fishing for striped bass at Lake Ouachita, which is a clear water impoundment in the rolling hills of southern Arkansas. It was the last day of the trip, and we had planned to pack up and begin the long drive back to Canada at about one in the afternoon. We had caught some nice largemouth bass and some Kentucky bass for the camera, as well as some big freshwater drum, but no stripers. We talked things over and elected to stay and fish until dark, knowing that, late in the day when the light is low, shad would come to the surface and get the stripers feeding.

Sure enough, this is exactly what happened. These huge, ferocious fish, which averaged about 10 pounds apiece, began ripping into shad

Bob with a dandy striper caught while filming in Arkansas with professional guide Hugh Albright. Paying attention to the needs of the fish paid off!

on or just under the surface. We ended up landing a number of stripers by burning Cotton Cordell Rattle Spots and slowly working big C-10 Redfins near the surface. It was the most exciting surface feeding-frenzy type of fishing I've ever seen in my life. And why was it so good? It was the same, textbook fish-were-following-the-baitfish scenario. We were able to capitalize on a basic fish need—food.

On other occasions shelter can be just as powerful an influence as food. I've won tournaments because my partners and I were able to find drop-offs, lily pads, reeds, boulders, and weedbeds the fish were using for shelter. In many cases, the fish were hiding in these areas to avoid predators. But in other instances, they were using them to ambush prey.

The third factor, comfort, is somewhat nebulous; but it has to do with factors such as water temperature and sunlight penetration. You can never forget that fish are cold-blooded animals. Because of this their movements will often be dictated, at least to a point, by water temperature. Since they can't control their own body temperatures, fish must travel to where things are most comfortable. This is why you normally find lake trout, which prefer cooler temperatures, on the bottom of a lake in 120 feet of water during the summer. That's where the cold water is.

Fish also don't have eyelids to protect themselves from the sun, nor do they have sunglasses like you and me. So when the sun shines brightly, look for fish to take cover in the shade—in thick weed patches, under lily pads, under logs or stumps, in the shadows of big rocks, or in deeper water where the light penetration is reduced.

If you consider the basic needs of fish, you'll be more selective about your fishing spots. And as a result, you'll catch more fish.

Best Days to Go Fishing

Tip 2

We recently videotaped a segment for the *Real Fishing* TV series on a good bass lake that, like most, gets a lot of fishing pressure on the weekends. On this particular weekday of taping, however, I caught a largemouth that weighed just a hair under seven pounds—the heaviest largemouth bass I've ever caught in Ontario. It hit a black and blue Riverside Big Claw that I had pitched under a tree located on a point—an obvious spot.

A fish such as this is probably in the mid- to high teens in age. In its life it has seen a lot of traffic and plenty of lures. The only way a bass lives this long on a heavily fished lake is by being elusive. On a normal weekend, the spot where I caught this bass might get hit three to six times. If there are a large number of serious anglers on the water, it might get fished this often in a day. So there's a good chance I would not have caught this bass if I had been there on a weekend. The fish would more than likely have been spooked out of there by fishing pressure or boat traffic.

The moral of the story is that although anytime is a good time to go fishing, certain days of the week can be far more productive than others. In fact, in some cases just picking the right day to go can be the most important decision an angler can make.

If you think about it for a moment, it's essentially a matter of considering fishing and boating pressure. Many of the more accessible lakes across the country lie close to big towns and cities. On weekends, there's a mass exodus of people to those watering holes to swim, boat, water ski, and, of course, fish.

All of this can add up to a carnival atmosphere on the water. With boat traffic overhead, it's not long before the fish develop lockjaw. For this reason, in the summer, Saturdays and Sundays can be the toughest days of the week to catch fish.

But there's a flip side to the coin. Thursdays and Fridays can be the best days of the week to head out onto the water. This is because, toward the end of the week, the fish calm down considerably and they're often much more aggressive.

Another thing, too, is that during the week you can often have the best locations all to yourself. You can work a slow finesse presentation in the tightest cover without being hassled or crowded out by the other boats.

Hey, go fishing anytime you can folks, but if you can beat the crowds by sneaking out before the weekend traffic, you could be in store for some incredible fishing.

Big Bait, Big Fish

Tip 3

If you want to catch big fish, and I mean those eye-popping, gigantic wall hangers, then use big baits and lures.

What's the biggest fish in your favorite lake? If it's pike or muskie, then check out the size of lures being fished these days by most good muskie and northern pike anglers. The plugs these guys throw are so big, they have to lug them around in ice coolers. Some of the baits are the size of your shoe—or better.

The "big bait, big fish" theory holds true whether you're trolling for walleye in Minnesota or casting for smallmouth in New Brunswick. In fact, out in Campbell River, British Columbia, two years ago, our guide motored up the coast for half an hour, just so he could buy some huge herring for bait. And talk about the size of live bait! While fishing for largemouth bass in Florida recently, our shiners were as big as some small stream trout you've seen anglers catch. Yet, fishing with these huge shiners, fishermen regularly pull out hawgs that weigh 8, 10, 12 pounds or better.

Even trout fishermen are getting into the act. Some fly fishing friends of mine recently discovered that their best patterns weren't tiny dry flies or nymphs, but huge, bushy deer-haired mice. In fact, these "flies" had been tied originally for bass and pike, but they turned out to be slayers for huge, trophy-sized speckled trout.

John Vandivier knows that big fish like big meals. Note the bizarre markings on his bruiser smallmouth. Biologists believe these are the fish equivalent of birthmarks.

Steve May, who works with me, regularly out-fishes other fly fishermen by catching huge brown trout on flies that would fill the palm of your hand—giant six- to eight-inch streamers. He says he caught onto the big fly patterns when he was working as a trout-fishing guide. He and a fellow guide were trying to catch a big pike that lived in a big, slow-moving river pool. This pike had attacked several trout their clients had hooked, so they went gunning for it with massive pike flies and salmon rods. They never got the pike, but they did catch a lot of big, aggressive brown trout that liked the look of the huge flies.

When I think of big baits, big fish, I think of my cohost of the *Real Fishing Radio Show*, Gord Pyzer. Gord catches record-sized muskies up in Northwestern Ontario by using very large crankbaits. Some of these massive lures are impossible to cast, which makes trolling the only option. A day of trolling with Gord definitely makes your arms about three feet longer because the big baits really pull. He doesn't use rod holders because he's trolling the lures around contours and around the edges of structures and he wants to feel the bait as it bounces up and down the rock breaks.

But does his technique work? You bet! Gord catches all kinds of huge muskies, and he's the only person I know who has released a potential 50-pound-plus muskie, plus several fish in the 40s. Can you imagine catching a muskie this large, taking a few photos, and then releasing it? It's obvious that he cares about the future of fishing, but he also knows how to catch fish.

Yet another example of the big bait, big fish scenario is the method of fishing for largemouth bass in Cuba. The most common bait there is a 9- to 12-inch black plastic worm. You would be amazed at how many 10- and 12-inch fish we catch on these giant worms, but my largest bass to date, an 11-pound-plus largemouth, was caught on a 12-inch black plastic worm.

So should you experiment with big baits? Absolutely! Don't be afraid to use seven-inch minnowbaits for walleye or big spinnerbaits for smallmouth or big crankbaits for brook trout. I know that some record catches have been made on small lures, but where consistency is concerned, big baits really do catch bigger fish.

Deking Them Out

Tip 4

There's an old saying that if the fishing is hot, then it's time to go prospecting, or to go looking for new fishing spots. For example, when there are a large number of boats working an area that's fairly dense with bait and salmon, often the guy who strays away from the crowd can catch more or bigger fish because he's got the fish all to himself. I've seen this happen on the ocean and on the Great Lakes, many times.

The old "boats attract boats theory," by which one boat appears then two, then three, is often more about people being inquisitive than about fish. I've seen good anglers caught up in this crazy way of boat traffic. If you're catching fish out in the open water and you throw a marker buoy way out, you might as well announce with a neon flashing light that you've got a red light special. The fact is that throwing out a marker buoy is the same as waving a sign "come and fish here."

If I'm catching fish and I'm concerned about my marker buoys attracting attention from other anglers, I'll go in a direction toward any landmarks, such as a silo, cottage, or point, and throw the marker off as much as a few hundred yards away on a spot on a featureless bottom. Then, using it as a reference, I'll come back to my original location. As the other boats start checking out my marker, I'll ease over to where the fish are really located. Another tactic is to throw a little piece of driftwood with a little piece of fishing line attached to it with a little bit of weight as a marker, because it seems that, depending on where you are fishing, there is different respect for marker buoys. For instance, I've found in upstate New York, on the Great Lakes, that if you throw a marker buoy out it's very common for resident anglers to come right around your buoys and fish. They regard the buoy as an open invitation. In Canada, fishermen respect markers and nobody goes around them, but the fact

If you're worried about competition from other anglers, position your marker buoys so they point the way to key spots, rather than setting them directly on the spots themselves, as most anglers do.

of the matter is you're inviting anglers when you throw a buoy out.

In a walleye tournament in Manitoba many years ago, my brother Wayne marked three hooks off a hump, threw out his buoy, caught a big walleye, and got back over it, but as he did, the other locals started to come in, eased over, and actually banged boats with Wayne (while they were all drinking a Texas Mickey). As they were making all the commotion the three hooks disappeared.

Another time, a fellow competitor, a friend of mine, was practicing before a tournament started. He found a paper coffee cup floating on the surface of the water and thought that it looked like it was anchored to something. He went up to it and found that there was a piece of fishing line and a heavy jig on the end of it, marking this point in a weedbed. He lowered down a jig and pig and caught about three giant bass. He proceeded to pick up the coffee cup and move it a few hundred yards off the point. He kind of knows whose cup it is, but he's not telling any secrets. Needless to say that guy had his work cut out for him the first morning of the tournament when he went back to his cup.

The worst thing is when people actually start catching fish around the buoy in an area you didn't even fish.

Doing Your Homework

Tip 5

All anglers are alike in one respect: we're always looking to learn more about fishing for our favorite species. Yet it still amazes me how some of the most obvious ways of learning about fishing are often overlooked. Buying fishing magazines, watching fishing shows, and listening to professional anglers at fishing seminars are all great ways to learn more about the sport. But what about just plain going fishing?

There's no question that I've learned more about fishing over the years by fishing with as many different anglers as possible. Granted, I'm in a great situation to do this. As a tournament angler and a TV fishing show host, I'm exposed to anglers from all over the world who use many different techniques. But this is how I've learned the most, bar none. Even before I got into this business, I always tried to fish with a number of different anglers: friends, acquaintances, and old-timers. In just one or two days of fishing with them, I was able to pick up tips that had taken them 25 to 30 years to figure out. Learning firsthand in this way, you remember what you learn, too.

Fishing guides are another great source of information. You can hire one practically anywhere in North America where there's water. A day of guided fishing will cost you some money, but when you consider the knowledge you'll learn, it's a great investment. I've fished with guides all around the world, and I'm always amazed at how what they've taught me creeps back into my day-to-day fishing back home.

Doing your homework also includes talking to people. I'm not recommending that you get your scalpel out and pick people's brains apart, but there's no harm in asking basic questions. At what depth are you catching the fish? Are you using crankbaits or live baits? Does it make a difference if the wind is blowing or not? Are you fishing rocks or weeds? These are all basic questions, but the answers can tell you a lot.

It's also a good idea to get yourself a good fishing map. Leo Capobianco, whom I met a number of years ago, had never fished before in his life, so I took him out fishing a few times and we became good friends. One day he decided to try ice fishing on his own. He went to a tackle shop and bought a fishing map that indicated the points, the shoals, and so on. He went up to Lake Scugog in central Ontario with one lure, half a fishing rod, and a dozen minnows. He went out on the lake and saw a guy ice fishing and asked him if he could borrow his auger. Then he walked several hundred yards away from the man he'd borrowed the auger from, drilled a hole, and returned the auger.

Although it was midday, and not exactly prime time for walleye, Leo ended up catching one over eight pounds, plus several other fish in about an hour or two of fishing. He knew nothing about ice fishing. Everyone he saw out on the ice afterward couldn't believe he'd caught fish when they hadn't caught anything.

Observing professional fishing guides like Jack Bauer of Tofino, BC, is one of the best ways to learn about fishing.

Luck? No, Leo had done his homework. For starters, he'd bought a chart to locate good structure for the fish. He knew fish liked points and areas where there's a change in the bottom. So once he'd located such a spot on the lake chart, that's where he drilled his hole. He only had one lure, but the one he took was an intelligent choice for what he was doing. I don't call this luck, I call it putting the odds in your favor. And how do you do this? You do your homework.

Effects of Warm and Cold Water

Most anglers know that fish are cold-blooded animals. But I wonder how many anglers really understand what this means. In a nutshell it means that the body temperature of a fish is not internally regulated; it approximates that of the environment and fluctuates accordingly.

For instance, during the winter when the water temperature is cold, say 40 degrees Fahrenheit, then this is roughly what the fish's internal body temperature is going to be. Of course, the opposite is true as well. If it's the middle of summer and the water is around 68 or 72 degrees Fahrenheit, any fish swimming in this warmer water are going to be roughly the same temperature.

The key point I want to make, then, is that every species of fish has a temperature range within which it feels comfortable. To simplify these ranges, biologists and anglers alike often refer to fish as being either cold-, cool-, or warm-water species. Knowing which category your

The warm-water outflows of hydro generating plants attract fish all winter long. Because the water temperature is artificially controlled, they're cold weather hot spots for a variety of species.

favorite fish falls into will tell you a lot about where you'll find it throughout the changing fishing season. And depending on the temperature of the water, you can quickly determine if the fish are going to be super active, or so sluggish they're almost impossible to catch.

Temperature preference also explains why warm-water fish, such as largemouth bass, are so hard to catch in frigid water. It's simply a case of their metabolism slowing down and making them as sluggish as maple syrup. A cold-water fish, such as lake trout, is almost the complete opposite. They actually enjoy water temperatures as chilly as 50 degrees Fahrenheit. This preference explains why trout migrate into the deeper reaches of a lake in the summer and also why they are active even under the ice in the winter.

All of this information is important to anglers. If the weather is hot and the water is warm, you should take advantage of the conditions and try to catch warm-water fish. Similarly, when things cool down and the weather conditions are no longer favorable for a warm-water species, go for a cool-water species instead. This is the benefit of fishing for a variety of different types of fish. No matter what time of year it is, it's perfect weather for at least one or two species.

But what if you really want to catch lake trout, for example, and it's 80 degrees in the shade? Well, you have to adjust your approach and find spots where the water temperature will be cold enough to keep lake trout alive and happy.

Some of the best lake trout fishing I've done, in fact, has been in midsummer. I try to fish the deepest area of the lake, where the temperature will be closest to the ice water lake trout prefer. This could be as much as 120 feet below the surface. I can't affect the weather, but I can decide to fish where conditions will be closest to what my target species finds most comfortable.

You can do just the opposite in the winter months if you live near a hydro generating station. Most hydro stations draw in water from a lake or river and use it to cool machinery, then pump the water back out several degrees warmer. In cold weather, the discharge areas off these hydro stations can provide great fishing for a variety of species. Everything from bass to walleye, from carp to rainbow trout will be attracted to these spots in the winter—all because of the warmer water.

In addition to depth, other things can affect water temperature. Shade, whether it's from water plants, such as lily pads, or from overhead trees or structures, such as docks, bridges, or culverts, is a big factor. Springs, though tough to locate, also have an effect upon water temperature within a small area. The inflowing water from tributary streams and creeks can either warm or cool things down. Even the shade of the bottom can have an effect. Shallow bays with dark bottoms, for instance, warm faster in the spring than those with light bottoms. A dark bottom holds heat from the sun, whereas a light bottom reflects more of this heat.

So, does water temperature have an effect upon your fishing success? You bet. Paying attention to water temperature can sometimes help you catch fish when things are not going well.

Estimating Weights

Tip 7

When I catch a big fish, the first question that usually comes to mind is, How much does it weigh? This is how most anglers judge fish—by weight. It's one thing to know you've just caught a really big walleye. But is it 10 pounds or only 9.5 pounds?

Fishermen have always attached qualities to fish associated with weight. What constitutes a trophy catch, for many people, is how much the fish weighs. In many regions, a 10-pound walleye is a real trophy, while an 8-pounder is just a really nice fish. This kind of evaluation is silly when you think about it, but it exists nevertheless.

If you don't have a scale in the boat, how do you estimate the weight of your catch? Hopefully, you have a tape measure on board, because the measurements of a fish can give you a good estimate of its weight.

Gord Pyzer, who cohosts the *Real Fishing Radio Show* with me, uses the following formula: multiply the fish's length by its girth, then multiply this number by the girth once again, and then divide by 800. The result is the approximate weight in pounds of your fish.

For example, if you catch a fish that is 40 inches long and has a 20-inch girth, multiply 40 times 20. The result is 800. Multiply 800 by another 20 and you get 16,000. Then, if you divide 16,000 by 800, you get 20. Bingo, your fish weighs approximately 20 pounds. It's that simple to calculate. And, if you forget your tape measure, that's no problem. Just cut one piece of fishing line the same length as the fish, and another piece the same length as the fish's girth. You can measure the pieces of line when you get home.

I'm always amazed at how some anglers can estimate the weight of fish with incredible precision. I know commercial fishermen who can call fish to within ounces of their actual weights. For example, an old-timer by the name of Floyd Cole (I'm not sure if he's really that old) and I have gone night fishing together on a number of occasions over the years, and Floyd can really guess the weight of giant walleyes. I've seen him hoist up 13.5-pound walleyes and be within an ounce of guessing their weight. He's done it too many times, and with fish of too many different sizes, for it to be just a lucky guess. Lately he claims his arm, I mean his scale, has been getting rusty with age.

Many tournament anglers are also good at estimating weights without using scales. Again, it's just

To estimate a fish's weight, multiply its length by its girth, multiply that amount by the girth again, then divide by 800. The result is the approximate weight in pounds.

by seeing enough fish over time, and knowing the actual weights of them, that your eye becomes trained. In fact, most of us like to underestimate the weight, so that when the scales flash the true number, it's a pleasant surprise.

I have some friends in the taxidermy business, and some of the fish they mount for customers actually weigh less than half of what the customer claims them to weigh. I know of several five-pound bass hanging on walls that, in truth, didn't pull an accurate scale to the five-pound mark. But the customer is always right, and good business people never argue.

Finding Current—and Fish

Current is very important to fish. It brings them food and oxygen, and gives them protection. If you find current, you'll generally find fish.

When most people think of current, they immediately picture a stream-fishing situation with trout and salmon. But current exists in lake fishing for warm-water species as well, not just in obvious ways, such as at lake narrows or at the base of waterfalls or at river mouths, but in more subtle ways too. Wind creates currents as it blows around points and islands, for example.

In my early years of fishing, I can remember spending time with Joe Stewart, fishing for bass on Rondeau Bay, a big bay located off the north shore of Lake Erie. Joe is a true bass fishing pioneer who has taught me a great deal about this sport, including how current affects the positioning and activity level of largemouth bass.

At Rondeau Bay, water either flows directly to the bay from Lake Erie, or directly from the bay to Lake Erie, depending on which way the wind is blowing. Whatever the resulting current, it drastically affects the positioning of the largemouth bass. Joe was legendary for catching dozens of largemouth bass in strategic locations—around breakwalls, rock areas, or weeds, just where the bass would be sitting facing into the flow.

Craig Ritchie is another guy who comes to mind when I think about current. Craig's a dyed-in-the-wool steelhead angler, and anytime from September till May, it's a good bet you'll find him knee-deep in water, chasing steelhead on some creek. And in the

Current is a magnet for almost all species of fish. Bob caught this nice muskie while fishing in a major current—the Niagara River, Ontario, above the falls—with guide Mark Counsell.

summer, when the steelhead are nowhere to be found, Craig just switches gears slightly, and fishes for smallmouth bass, walleye, and channel catfish—sometimes in the same spots where he fishes for steelhead, occasionally with the same tackle and techniques. He knows that current affects these species in the same way it affects steelhead.

Whether the current is formed by wind or by a river situation, remember your first cast is the most important cast. I've never seen any fish sit tailfirst into a current. They always face the flow head-on, and often the biggest and best fish will be the one right at the front of the line, where it gets first shot at any food that drifts by. It's best to cast slightly up-current of where you think the fish are and let the water flow direct your bait to them naturally.

Then, hold on. If your cast is good and the fish are there, you'll usually get a hit right away. The fish that sit in current aren't shy at all. So, next time you're on the water, look for signs of current and use these signs to your advantage. Currents are fish magnets everywhere.

Fish Activity Levels

Tip 9

Fish are moody creatures. The secret to enjoying steady fishing action really does lie in knowing their moods. Generally speaking, fish are either in an active, neutral, or negative mood. These terms, or moods, are known as fish activity levels. And being aware of them is extremely important. So critical, in fact, that they should dictate the lure and type of presentation that you use.

For example, imagine there are some big old bass lurking in a cabbage bed. If these fish are really active, swimming high in the water and feeding aggressively, your best approach is a rapid one, like buzzing a spinnerbait or buzzbait over the weed tops, or burning a rattlebait, such as a Cordell Spot, along the weedline. In other words, when the fish are aggressive, your presentation should be fast paced as well.

But, let's say these same bass are in a negative or neutral mood. You have to change your strategy. In this case, reach for a lure that you can fish slowly, deep down along the bottom.

Just because these fish are inactive doesn't mean they can't be caught. But, usually, you must slow down your retrieve and drag your lure right across their noses to tantalize them into striking.

So, rather than the fast-moving spinnerbait, fish a Texas-rigged plastic worm or jig and pig combination instead, moving very slowly along the bottom.

If there was ever a moody fish invented it would have to be good ol' mister walleye. This past fall I had the best night fishing of my life for walleye—11 fish landed, 2 small ones that weighed about 4.5 pounds apiece, another 1 at about 8 pounds, 4 medium-sized ones at 10 pounds apiece, and 4 giants that weighed between 13 and 14 pounds each. These walleyes were caught by slow trolling Smithwick deep-diving Rogue minnowbaits and Rebel Spoonbill minnowbaits. The key was to be very slow with the electric motor so as not to spook the fish and to keep that slow wobbling action in the deep-diving minnowbait.

On this particular evening we got out to do some night taping and the first fish was an eight-pounder. But we didn't bring all the right audio equipment in the boat with us, so we had to run a mile and a half back in the pitch black night to the Suburban at the boat ramp to get the proper microphones and cables. Once we got back out on the water, the next fish was pushing 14 pounds. We fished until about two that morning, and needless to say it's a night I'll never forget.

Obviously, we hit those walleyes during a very high activity level. For starters, we were fishing at night when walleye feed most heavily. The other thing is, these fish were herding shad in shallow water flats, weed edges, bays, on top of shoals. Needless to say, they were greedily pigging out.

During the day you could troll these same areas that I fished and probably not catch any walleye at all. But that's the point—the bright sun of daylight puts these particular walleye into a low activity level.

To catch more and bigger fish, try to be on the water when fish activity peaks. This comes down to learning as much as you can about the fish you're trying to catch, then getting on the water when conditions are best.

Fish Scents

At the seminars I've presented at various sportsmen's shows across the country, it's easy to remember the most frequently asked questions. And one that screams to the top of the list is: Are fish scents a gimmick?

There's no question about it—commercial attractants aren't tricks to make us spend money. As far as I'm concerned, they help.

This is true for a couple of reasons. First, remember that fish can be in one of three different moods or levels of activity: inactive, neutral, or active. Now when they're inactive or neutral, which is most of the time, they're not really thinking about eating. So dabbing a little bit of artificial scent on your lure can be just the ticket for stimulating their appetite.

This is especially true during the colder periods of the year. The reason is simple—in cold water, fish react more slowly to everything. It takes them longer to check out your offering. If your lure both looks good and smells good, they will be more likely to pick it up.

Attractants work on two different levels. First, they mask the human odor that lingers on our lures. Most fishermen don't realize it, but there's a natural oily substance on our fingers called L-serine, which has been proven to repel most species of fish. When you add in other odors that might be on our hands, such as gas, oil, or tobacco, then there's just more for fish to consider before eating our baits. If a lure smells foreign, chances are the fish will be less inclined to eat it. In fact, you can read of numerous experiments in which researchers diluted minute quantities of L-serine in gallons and gallons of water, and then added the mixture to fish tanks in a hatchery. And do you know what happened? The fish went berserk.

The second reason for using attractants is that, in some cases, they actually contain naturally enticing odors. Real Craw, for example, is one attractant I use often in bass fishing because it's made of real crayfish oils. This particular attractant does more than simply mask human odors—it really works as an enticement, triggering bass to feed.

Many of the oil-based attractants can also work as lubricants for your artificial lures. When I'm fishing soft plastic worms, crayfish, tubes, and lizards in cover, a freshly applied oil-based scent helps. The lubricated baits will easily slip through the lily pads, reeds, weeds, and wood directly to where the fish live.

When we either cast or slow-troll plugs for nighttime walleye, we religiously apply an attractant such as Real Baitfish. I feel an attractant is especially important for lures that are used slowly. With an attractant the fish really gets a chance to check the lure out.

Scents can also give fishermen a boost in confidence. Many years ago at a Pro Bass tournament on Big Rideau Lake in eastern Ontario, I located a big bass near a tree off an island. After catching a limit in a weedbed I pulled up to this tree, looked down, and saw a five-pounder sitting in the very same spot as the day before. I grabbed a weedless tube jig and proceeded to try to catch this very big bass. After a few minutes of no interest, I reeled the tube in and gave it a good squirt of Real Craw. I lowered the tube down in front of the bass and, within seconds, the bass inhaled the bait.

So do scents make sense? I always say that they can't do any harm. And when I'm fishing in a big money bass tournament or, worse yet, am under pressure to produce fish for the television camera, I do everything I can to put the odds in my favor. For my money, attractants work.

Getting Hooks Out

Tip 11

Let me set the record straight. I've been in the fishing business now for over 20 years full-time. For the first dozen years or so of my career I had never hooked myself past the barb in my life. Sure I've had hook points in my hand—that's an everyday occurrence. But my perfect record of never stabbing myself past the barb was ruined about 10 years ago.

At the time I was doing a trout fishing trip, filming rainbows by using long noodle rods with floats and night-crawlers and letting them bob and drift with the wind. One day it was quite windy and with the long noodle rod I carefully tried to cast into the wind. These were long rods—11.5 feet long—and we had long leads under our floats, probably eight or nine feet anyway. As I unleashed a cast into the wind, the long lead under my float got caught in the wind. The hook swung around and nailed me right in the cartilage on the front part of my ear. The number six hook stuck there, well past the barb.

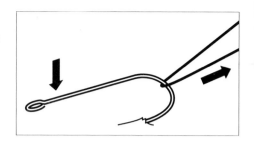

The good thing is, I was able to pull the night-crawler off so that it didn't squirm around in my ear. But here I am with a hook embedded in my head. In such a situation, what do you do, just yank out the hook with pliers? As it happened, we couldn't pull it out—it was in a tender spot. So we ended up driving into the hospital in town. The doctor gave me a local anesthetic and he pulled it out.

To get a hook out of your skin, press down on the eye while pulling straight back with a fishing line or a wire leader looped around the hook bend. If it doesn't pop out easily, don't force it. Get medical attention, pronto.

A few years prior to this incident I'd filmed a tip on emergency hook removal with my sister, Lynn, who is a medical doctor. Lynn used a grapefruit for the tip, as it was hard to find a live volunteer. One of her techniques involved putting pressure on the opposite side of the barb, by pressing the shank of the hook against the bend in the hook, and popping it out with a piece of fishing line. Trust me—it's much easier to perform this technique on grapefruits than it is on humans.

The second time I got hooked was in New York State. I was taping for the TV series on Lake Erie and catching some monster small-mouth, some weighing over six pounds. Every now and then, I also caught the occasional perch, and at this particular moment I had a jumbo of about a pound and a half on my spinning rod line. After a big breakfast, however, I was too lazy to bend down and grab it. So, I thought I'd just lift it over the side and grab it, as I had done with hundreds of other perch in my life.

Well, while the perch was in midair, with my spinning rod loaded up and all kinds of tension on the line, the jig came flying out of the perch's mouth and went sailing right into my baby finger, barb nowhere to be seen. I didn't really want to take the time with it, because the smallmouth were biting, so I just yanked it out with a set of pliers. It hurt like blazes. Now, I did it the wrong way folks—I used pliers and yanked the hook out because the fishing had to go on. I don't recommend you do that.

This misadventure was just the beginning. Later the following year I had a hooking incident on Lake St. Clair while fishing at a Pro Bass tournament. I was working a spinnerbait in fairly shallow water and I got a hit. I missed the fish though, and the spinnerbait came rocketing out of the water, spiraling in midair, and, of course, the hook sunk into my shin. It was a big 3/0 hook and it went in way past the barb. I was so upset that I had missed the fish, primarily because we still didn't have a limit yet in the livewell, that I grabbed the pliers and just ripped the hook out, much to my partner's shock. He asked me if I wanted help, but at that point I wanted fish, not assistance.

You think that would be enough, wouldn't you? Nope. Couple of years ago I was down in Florida fishing in the phosphate pits for large-mouth bass and filming a segment with Chad Spence from Strike King Lures. We were using the new Denny Brauer pro rattling jig, built on a giant 5/0 hook with a huge barb. I got a bass of about three pounds on it and lifted it into the boat with my heavy flipping tackle. Remember the Lake Erie perch? You'd think I would learn, right? You guessed it—as I got the bass about two feet off the surface of the water, the jig comes flying out of its mouth, the heavy rod recoils with all its power, and that great big 5/0 hook comes screaming back at me at something just this side of the speed of sound. I had my hand stretched out to grab the fish and—presto—the hook's embedded in the skin between my index finger and thumb. We're back in good ol' boy country of central Florida, way back in a pasture fishing in a pit. And, the fish are on, big-time. I don't want to leave, but this doesn't look good.

Now, because he grew up around his dad's lure factory in Tennessee, Chad has watched hundreds of people get hooked over the years with Strike King lures. He says great, he'll show me a foolproof way of removing the lure. It's the same fishing line trick Lynn had used on the grapefruit. He put the fishing line in the bend of the hook and started to pull it with all his might, but he couldn't even budge the hook. I looked at him and said, "Chad, just get the pliers."

Chad is a strong guy, so when he started hauling on this hook with the pliers, he yanked my hand all over the place. I guess by then I was putting up a pretty good fight, too. Finally I braced myself with my other hand, planted my feet on the floor of the boat, and told him to pull as hard and as fast as he could. I thought he was going to rip my fingers off, but he finally got the hook out. My hand felt numb at first, but we continued fishing, and I think we caught about 40 fish that day after the hook incident. Just another day at the office.

My only experience with anybody getting a hook out of any part of their body other than the shins, hands, or ears was with Gord Pyzer fishing on Great Bear Lake in the Northwest Territories for trophy lake trout back in the 1980s. Great Bear is about as remote as it gets, and the fishing is just unbelievable.

We were shooting underwater video of some lures after we had finished catching a number of fish for a show segment. The camera crew was wading in the shallow water with the underwater camera, while I was casting and retrieving the bait in front of the lens. That's when they asked for a slightly longer cast than I had been making. I didn't know

Gord was right behind me, so when I wound up for the cast, I snagged him right on top of the head. Now, we have a deal within our company—if anybody gets hooked, cameraman, guest, or anybody, they get to keep the bait. The positive thing is that Gord got to keep my lure. The negative thing was that we couldn't get the lure out. We returned to the lodge, Gord wearing this thing like a hat. A woman, who said she was a nurse, came to help Gord. With a pair of pliers, she cut the lure off. But she cut so close to the top of his skull that the rest of the hook just sank right in. As a result, the skin swelled around the little stub of hook so that it couldn't be grasped with the pliers. And this was only the start of the fishing trip!

We could have flown Gord out to a small medical center at a local native reserve, but he didn't want to miss out on any of the fabulous fishing. So, for the remainder of the trip, he had to sleep in a sitting position on the corner of his bed. At the end of the week, when we got back to Edmonton, we took Gord to a hospital and they removed the rest of the hook. I think he still has a little bald spot on the top of his head where I gave him that lure, but at least he is up one bait.

Getting Started in Tournament Fishing

Tip 12

There's no question that you can learn more about fishing by entering a competitive tournament. If nothing else, tournaments force you to be out on the water for eight hours a day for up to three straight days under changing conditions, and you simply have to produce. It can be the ultimate crash course in fishing.

The ProAm tournaments, which I'm very fond of, can be a great way to learn more about fishing generally and to get your feet wet in competitive fishing. As an amateur in one of these events, you can draw local or big name pros as your daily partner, giving you an opportunity to see firsthand how other people catch fish. And, because you're in a tournament with big prizes up for grabs, they're not going to hold anything back. You learn all their best tricks.

Even better, the entry fee for these events is normally much less than what you would pay a top-notch guide for just one day on the water, much less two or three days.

Tournament fishing is a great way to learn because you're out there under all conditions. I've fished ProAm tournaments since the late '80s, and it's unbelievable now how some of my top competitors today

Waiting for blastoff at the start of a tournament can be one of the most exciting experiences in competitive fishing.

started out as amateurs in these events. By being able to pick the brains of various anglers from different regions, they were able to fast-track it into the world of competitive tournament fishing. Whereas some of us might have taken 25 years to develop a technique, they learned it in a day.

There are probably 200 or 300 tournament fishing organizations in North America, and they're not all focused on bass. There are pike tournaments, walleye tournaments, muskie tournaments, and panfish tournaments. Getting started in tournaments is easier now than it ever was.

My dad, the late Joe Izumi, ran the first bass tournament in Canada. I still have the poster at home that boasts "Over $300 in prizes." Today, that's a very low prize, even in smaller tournaments.

It's surprising how tournament fishing attracts people from all walks of life. Your daily partner could be just about anybody. I once fished in a ProAm tournament with NHL hockey star Bryan Marchment, who plays defense for the San Jose Sharks. It wasn't going well, and we only had a 9- or 10-pound limit for the day. Finally, in the last hour and a half, we got into some better quality fish. At one point I watched Brian unhooking a three-pound smallmouth. His hands were shaking and I asked him if he was all right. He said that, even with all his years of playing professional hockey, the adrenaline rush from tournament fishing was incomparable.

That's why I love tournament fishing—the exhilaration is incredible. If you've ever wondered what it's like, try a ProAm event. Even if you decide afterward that this type of event is not for you, there's no doubt you'll come away a better angler.

Handling Big Fish

I recently watched a television fishing show about muskie. Of course, the host, who's a pretty good angler, caught a very nice muskie for the camera. Now, his intentions were good and his message about catch-and-release was excellent. But the trouble was, the whole time he was talking, the muskie was dangling from a gaff.

If you held your breath from the moment this fish was landed, you would be gasping for air long before it was ever put back into the water. It wasn't the *Real Fishing Show*, because as you know, we're careful about handling and protecting fish.

But the fact is, many anglers don't realize that fish can suffocate out of the water. It's no different than you or me being held underwater for a prolonged period of time. Like a fish out of water, we wouldn't be able to breathe. Held there long enough, we could suffer brain damage or even die.

And don't forget that the big fish you've just landed has expended a tremendous amount of energy. It's gasping for breath when you bring it in the boat. So, think of it this way—you just ran a marathon, as fast as you can, you're gasping for breath, and at the finish line, someone holds your head underwater.

This is why the ideal situation for fish you plan to release is to not remove them from the water. Just reach over the side, remove the hook with as little fuss as possible, and send the fish on its merry way.

If you want to hold the fish up for a picture, make sure you properly support its body. Bass can be held by the lower jaw, providing you let the fish hang straight down. But don't use the lower jaw as a lever because this will overextend it. Large trout, salmon, muskie, pike, and walleye can be held by gripping them with one hand carefully under the gill covers. If possible, use your other hand to support the fish elsewhere. Holding the fish horizontally is the best approach of all. If you intend to take a number of photos, you can rest the fish in an aerated livewell for a few minutes before continuing.

The guides at Great Bear Lake in the Northwest Territories really know how to handle those giant lake trout. Lake trout are slow-growing fish, and it takes decades for them to reach trophy proportions. Lakers are also fairly fragile fish, and as slippery as greased pigs. When it comes time to lift a fish out of the water for a photo, the Great Bear guides cradle their fish horizontally, using their forearms to

Great Bear Lake guides, such as Ryan Haines and Brien Morgan, know how to carefully handle big fish—by always supporting the fish's body weight.

support the weight of these massive trout, which can reach as much as 65 pounds.

If you are careful handling the fish, they stand an excellent chance of survival. Countless studies have been conducted on tournament-caught bass and walleyes that demonstrate this. Although it is controversial how many released fish survive, my opinion is that the vast majority of properly handled fish do just fine.

I see evidence of this all the time, when I catch fish that have healed scars on their jaws. Perhaps the best example of multiple catch-and-release that I've witnessed occurred in 1998, when I was competing in the Kenora Bass International Tournament with Craig Ritchie. We were fishing on the final day of the three-day event held on beautiful Lake of the Woods, on the Ontario-Manitoba border. Craig was using a Rebel Pop R surface bait when he saw a three-pound-plus bass suspended just under his bait, looking at it, and all of a sudden the bass came up and sucked the bait in as if it was a bug on the surface. Upon landing that fish, which was our largest fish of the day, we saw it had a gray spaghetti tag sticking out just beneath its dorsal fin. After we weighed in that day, Craig asked one of the Ontario Ministry of Natural Resources biologists who were collecting scale samples from weighed-in bass about that particular tag. It turned out that fish was caught by another angler on the first day of the tournament, transported to Kenora in the angler's livewell, weighed in alive in front of a huge crowd of people, and then transported more than 20 miles away from town and released. Then, when Craig caught it again on day three, it went through the same trip all over again. The amount of miles that fish traveled should have qualified it for some frequent flyer points.

Joking aside though, it really showed that catch-and-release does work if you handle the fish carefully.

How to Land a Fish

Tip 14

It's often called the moment of truth. You lean over the side of your boat to see how big your fish is, and your net feels as though it weighs a hundred pounds. All you can think is, "Lord, don't let me blow it now."

As long as you follow a few basic rules, you can put the odds in your favor for not losing a fish at the side of your boat. One thing to remember is to keep your rod tip high, with at least a rod-length's worth of line between it and the fish. This lets you handle any last-ditch rushes the fish might decide to make.

And using the proper landing equipment is also important. A net is usually the best device for most fish. But over the years I've seen some comical situations where fishermen have tried to land big fish with nets that were too small, were too short in handle length, or had too many holes in the mesh.

Another cardinal rule is to always net your fish headfirst. Never come at it from behind. If you try to net a fish tail-first and you happen to touch it, the fish will panic and swim away from the net. But, if you net it head-first, it will be swimming right into the mesh.

And whatever else happens, don't panic. If the fish has a bit more strength left, then let it swim around for a second or two longer before you try to net it. Just don't go dipping and splashing at it wildly, because you're likely to miss it and accidentally jar it free.

The fact is, no matter how good you are, you're going to make mistakes and lose fish, but there are ways of landing fish both with and without nets. On a recent muskie taping session, we got out on the water on the last day of the season in central Ontario. I forgot to bring a suitable net for landing muskies.

Needless to say, it was a memorable day of muskie fishing. I was with Carlo Alessandrini, a friend from bass tournament fishing. Carlo had never fished for muskie specifically but had caught some by accident while fishing for bass over the years. I thought it would be fun if he and I shot a muskie show together.

Always net a fish head-first. This way, should the fish panic, it will simply drive itself further into the mesh.

We got out on the water on the last day of the season and it was brutally cold. The line guides on our rods were freezing up, but we ended up with a total of 12 muskies. We lost two, but we boated three that weighed between 15 and 25 pounds. Not giants, but decent-sized muskie anywhere. The key here was, how do you land a good-sized muskie without a net?

Well, it's obvious that when you grab them, you'd better get a good grip; if not, you risk getting some big hooks in the hand or forearm. Because the water was cold on that particular day and the fights were reasonably short, landing the fish amounted to taking a good look at them in the water first. If the fish was hooked on the right side of the mouth, we would gently slide our hand under the gill plate on the left side of the fish's head and grab it there firmly at the water's surface, then lift it up with the other hand supporting its weight. It worked out just fine—sometimes it's nice to forget some of the so-called necessities of fishing.

On another occasion, while filming a salmon fishing segment at Owen Sound, Ontario, in early April, my partner and I once again forgot to bring a net. Owen Sound is about a two-and-a-half-hour drive from our office, and we absolutely had to be on the water at dawn for the best fishing. In order to meet, get our stuff together, get the video equipment packed, and stop for a coffee, we had to be up at two in the morning. That we forgot something as basic as the net was no big surprise.

I have to tell you that reaching into ice water to grab chinook salmon was not fun, but by taking our time and being careful, we had no problems.

Landing fish without a net is much easier if you're not in a boat. When you're stream fishing or casting from shore, you can usually find a spot to beach your fish. Beaching works like magic—you lead the fish into shallow water and when it feels the bottom under it, it will try to swim. As long as you keep its head facing the right way, it will push itself up high and dry, more often than not.

Landing fish is even easier when you're fishing from shore or stream fishing. Then, you can just select a spot with a gently sloping shoreline and beach the fish.

If no such spot exists, then you have to improvise. Grabbing fish by hand works just as well from shore as it does from a boat. Take your time and you should have few problems. Bass are the easiest to handle—just grab them by the lower lip. When dealing with toothy critters, such as pike, muskie, or large walleye, use one hand to grab them just in front of the tail, then use your other hand to grab them under the belly, toward the gill covers. This also works very well with salmon and trout.

Walleye and smaller pike can be grabbed by spanning your hand over their backs, just behind the head, and by placing your fingers over the outside of the gill covers.

How Wind Affects Fish

Tip 15

Windy weather can bring great fishing. Many anglers use the term "walleye chop" to describe how wind attracts these particular fish. And some anglers know that a bit of a breeze can do good things for pike and muskie. But wind can make great fishing for many other species of fish as well.

Wind affects fish because it pushes water around, forming currents where none existed before. This, in turn, creates feeding opportunities for fish.

Moving water means moving algae and plankton, so small fish waste no time in positioning themselves straight in the path of the current so that they can effortlessly intercept this parade of food drifting by. The rolling waves also offer protection from overhead predators such as birds, giving these small fish the chance to feed without continually scanning the skies for danger. This also applies to game fish as well. Walleye, for instance, are more likely to move shallow in windy weather because the wave action cuts light penetration to levels that give them a predatory advantage. Big fish feel safer in the shallows when there's a wind blowing.

Wind-induced waves pounding against a shoreline provide a number of bonus food items for predatory fish as well. Waves dislodge crayfish, frogs, newts, and all sorts of other creatures that may ordinarily be difficult to catch, so for the predators, wind is a doubly good thing.

Wind blowing across a lake helps to narrow your choice of filming locations. The best are places where the wind blows full-force onto points, reefs, or saddles, or where there is softer cover such as weed mats, because chances are fish are near these areas to begin with. What the wind does is haul the fish off the bottom and out of the cover, and put them up into relatively shallow, open water where you can catch them more easily.

Fish that are feeding actively will position themselves on the upwind side of the cover or structure, where they get first crack at any potential prey. Fishing these areas with reaction baits, such as spinnerbaits or lipless crankbaits, can result in tremendous action. Burning a big tandem-blade spinnerbait, such as a Strike King Premier Elite, or a rattling lipless crankbait, such as a Cordell Spot, along windswept points and saddles is always a good strategy no matter where you fish or what species you're trying to catch.

If it's windy, you should target windswept points, saddles, and shorelines with reaction baits.

As an example, I set out late one day last summer to tape a segment on smallmouth bass. As it happened, the wind was blowing hard, so hard that I began to wonder if we would be able to shoot. The wind doesn't bother me, but the sound of it ripping over the wireless microphone can make the audio unusable.

We went out anyway, and wound up having a great time catching smallmouth bass, which weighed up to four pounds, by pounding big spinnerbaits along rocky shorelines. The bass were very aggressive and prowled very shallow water, so as soon as they hit, they became airborne. It was a great segment.

I can remember a similar experience that occurred many years ago while fishing at Lac Nitchequin in north central Quebec with Jerry Moon, a friend of mine from Texas. We were on the last day of the trip and wanted to get a good lake trout segment, as Jerry had never had much opportunity to fish for lake trout before. Once again, the wind was howling so hard I was concerned that it would roar through the microphones and make the tape tough to work with. But we were miles from nowhere and had nothing to lose. We went out anyway.

Not coincidentally, Jerry and I were fishing almost exactly the same way as I was on the smallmouth shoot—by pounding windswept points. The only difference was that instead of a spinnerbait, we were throwing ½-ounce Cordell Spots. And, instead of using a Ranger bass boat, we were in a small aluminum boat, as it was a very remote fly-in lodge. But other than that, the fishing was very similar, even though it was for a completely different species in a different lake 1,000 miles away.

So, it doesn't matter where you live or what you're fishing for. Wind can be a good thing. Of course, play it safe if it's rough and use some common sense. Try casting reaction baits along windswept structures and you could be in for some incredible action.

Kneeling and Reeling

Tip 16

"If only I could get my crankbaits to dive down an extra foot or so. Boy, could I catch fish then!"

This is a comment I've heard more than once. Many fishermen are surprised to learn that there is a simple method for getting extra depth from their crankbaits. It's called kneeling and reeling.

Let's say you're casting a big, wide-lipped crankbait that normally dives down to about 12 feet in depth. But, the fish are in 15 or 16 feet of water, and not interested in coming shallower. What do you do?

Instead of holding your rod as you would normally, with the tip perhaps head-height, point it straight down so your tip is in the water. This will drop your bait by about five feet or more. And don't worry about not being able to feel hits—this won't be a problem.

If that still doesn't give you enough extra depth, then literally get down on your knees and plunge your rod tip farther into the lake. You just bought yourself a few extra feet.

Spooling up with thin diameter line also helps gain a little extra depth. Thin line has less resistance as it passes through the water, letting your bait dive deeper.

When I think of kneeling and reeling, I think of my buddy Blaine Schmidt, who is a CFL veteran. Blaine appeared with me in a Shimano television commercial for their Carbomax rods—he was the big guy on the Harley, who lifted me out of my bass boat when I snagged my lure on his bike. Anyway, one day as we shared a boat on central Ontario's Lake Simcoe, he told me about catching a lot of fish on light line crankbait fishing. So, we went out and did a little kneeling and reeling. I'll never forget seeing this six-foot-three, 300-plus-pound man fishing beside me in the bow of the boat, kneeling and reeling to catch large-mouth and smallmouth bass. I never got much of a suntan that day, as I was always fishing in Blaine's shadow!

Knowing When to Change

Old Joe Stewart from Blenheim, Ontario, who taught me about fishing in my early years, was my tournament partner for the first-ever Rice Lake Bass Tournament back in the late 1970s. We were leading the pack of 150 teams after the first day, after catching about 40 bass on buzzbaits over one weedbed that was probably three acres in size. Ironically, this was a spot we found only in the last hour or so of five straight days of practice fishing.

The second day of the tournament, Joe and I were revved up; we thought we would easily win it. Meanwhile, my brother Wayne and his partner, Mark Little from Kentucky, were in ninth place; it looked as if they'd finish in the top 10. We immediately went back to the same area with the intention of catching another good limit on buzzbaits.

Well, we buzzed for about four hours and got precisely one hit. After three or four more hours of throwing these things, we had zip to show for it. Apparently we had stayed too long with the previous day's successful technique. Finally, we decided to fish the weedbeds with slow moving baits. We used a jig and pig and plastic worms.

When things just aren't going right, they're seriously not going right. Joe and I proceeded to lose about half a dozen quality fish by using this slow, deep technique. It got so bad that after we lost a number of big bass, I said, "Remember that log that was just over on that shoreline? Remember on Thursday during pre-fish I caught a three-and-a-half-pound bass under it? Let's go back to that log."

We went back to the log and I threw a plastic worm alongside it. I felt a little hit so I set the hook. But, unfortunately, I lost the fish halfway to the boat. So here we are with no fish in the boat and less than an hour to go before weigh-in time. We decided to go out on a weedline and started to fish with plastic worms. We caught a couple of little bass, but our weigh-in was dismal, and we dropped down to ninth place in the tournament, just where Wayne and Mark had been the day before. Their second day had gone much better than ours—they caught some big bass in the cabbage weed patches by fluttering chartreuse spinnerbaits through the cabbage. The technique involved killing their lures so that they would flutter down into the stalks. Their weight was good enough and they ended up winning the tournament. I guess the moral of the story is to know when it's time to change techniques.

To catch fish, especially in tournaments or any time there are a lot of other anglers on the water, it's important to be versatile in your approach. There are two schools of thought on knowing when to change. If you're fishing a lake you know well, and you're on a spot that you know holds fish, you have the luxury of being able to switch your approach freely. When I fish tournaments now, I sometimes have 12 to 18 rods in the boat, all rigged with different lures and line weights, and I don't hesitate to switch from a crankbait to a jig if I'm confident fish are using the spot.

It's a different story if you're prospecting though. If you're trying out a new lake for the first time, and you don't know for certain that fish are actually using the spot you're fishing, it's probably best to hang in there and try a few more locations before deciding to switch tactics.

For years I have found that when the fish are active and hitting your tried-and-true lures, this is the best time to change and experiment. This is when you can switch to lures you haven't had success with before. Talk about a confidence booster when they start to work!

Learning from Fishing Guides

Tip 18

If you want to become a better fisherman, there is no substitute for time on the water. That's the difference between the weekend angler and the professional guide who is fishing five or six days a week. The guide who's out there almost daily is in tune with what's going on and knows the fish's movements. The easiest way to become more successful is to hire fishing guides and to learn from them.

The information you can glean from guides can concern equipment, line size, lure weights, colors, designs or types, and location of fish. In many cases this information is going to be as important as your fishing technique. Attention to fine details can make all the difference.

One thing I don't recommend is to hire fishing guides for the purpose of learning all their spots. That's not fair to them, and in reality you're not learning anything if you take that approach. Instead of memorizing their spots so that you can go back and fish them, learn why their spots are good, then use that knowledge to go find your own.

The best guides realize that they have to be good with people. They have to read your mind at the beginning of the day to figure out what it is you really want. These are the guys who make money in tips, because, at the end of the day, they have given you what you want. Catching fish is only part of it.

Over the years some of the guides I've met have been real characters. I can remember a native Indian from the north who used to guide visiting anglers. Throughout the course of the day he'd take his hat off and wipe his brow, then look up at the sky, study it for a while, and accurately guess the time of day. In fact, he was always right, give or take two or three minutes. The visitors were in awe of this guy. They would go back to their lodge and brag about how their guide was so in touch with nature.

What they didn't know was that the guide had taped one of those little 99-cent digital clocks to the inside of his hat. So every time he pulled his hat off and wiped his brow, he could sneak a peek at the clock. Staring up at the sky was just an act. He made a lot of money in tips over the years with his trick of the trade.

I can remember being with another native Indian guide, working our way slowly up the coast in a small boat. He pointed to a rock on the shore and said, "You see that rock over there?" I nodded, expecting to be told something significant about it. Maybe it marked a fishing spot; perhaps it had spiritual significance. Perhaps there was an eagle nest there.

Nope. He looked at me, glanced at the rock, and said, "Yup, that's been there for a long time."

Hiring a guide is a great way to learn about fishing, but it's also a great way to simply have fun on the water—and that's the whole point.

Professional fishing guides like David Murphy of Port Alberni, BC, know it isn't enough to simply catch a lot of fish. Guides must be able to read their customers in order to do whatever it takes to make their day on the water a special and memorable experience.

Mental Preparation and Confidence

Tip 19

I've fished competitive tournaments since I was about 15, and over the years I've always got a kick out of talking to fellow competitors, when they come up and tell me what an awful practice they had, that they didn't catch any fish, or that they didn't get any patterns going. They're already beating themselves up before the competition even starts. Chances are these people will never win a tournament if they're negative about their chances of catching fish.

There is no question that confidence plays a very large role in successful fishing. First of all you have to tell yourself that fish are not smarter than you are. It's nice to talk about fish intelligence, but let's keep things in perspective—even the brightest fish have brains the size of a breath mint!

When you're out on the water, try to be logical and keep your cool.

Remember that fish, like humans, have basic needs: food, shelter, and comfort. By studying up on the species of fish you're trying to catch, you can find out where they feed and where they live on a given body of water. Next, you must determine if the fish are hungry or not. If they're not hungry, it's going to be slow fishing.

The best anglers I've fished with around the world, whether they're charter captains, fishing guides, tournament anglers, or just experts in their fishing field, are all alike in one key respect—they're all very positive in their approach. I was recently fishing with a guide who had worked 137 days straight without a day off. He was telling me that every day he goes out there, he feels like today is the day; it's going to be great. He's often right, and it's that mental preparation that puts him in a position to enjoy great action.

In the early years of tournament angling, my brother Wayne and I would be disappointed if we didn't win every tournament we entered. I guess you could call that cocky or overconfident, but our attitude probably made all the difference. Confidence allowed us to keep our heads screwed on when things weren't going well at all. On many occasions we had no fish in the livewell or a very small catch, then we caught a pile of bass in the final moments of the competition and won. This won't happen if you think you're beat from the beginning.

Mental preparation also has an effect when things are going well. It can make the difference between a good day on the water and a great one. In one tournament on central Ontario's Kawartha Lakes, Wayne and I had a limit of fish in the livewell that would have probably placed us in the top 10. But in the last 10 minutes of fishing, we caught a couple of four-pound bass that essentially won the tournament for us. We kept trying right till the end and it paid off.

On another occasion, while fishing Lake St. Clair during one of the early South Western Ontario Bass Association, or SWOBA, tournaments with John Vandivier, I hooked a smallmouth bass about 10 inches long right in the final moments of the last day. As I brought it to the boat I looked down and saw that there were four other fish following my little one. I yelled for John to throw down another bait, but in the excitement his gear got tangled up. I was crying and laughing inside because I knew these fish were eager to hit and that we might be able to catch them.

Seeing that John was having problems, I handed him my rod with the little bass on it, calmly reached down, grabbed a rod with a jig on it, and flipped in a cast. I managed to catch every fish in that school except the very biggest one. So I grabbed another rod with a split shot rig, flipped it out, and dragged it on bottom. By this time, the wind had slowly pushed us almost 80 yards from where we'd initially hooked the first little bass. I felt a tick, but the smallmouth was so far away from the boat I could barely see it. I set the hook and a four-pounder came out of the water and broke my line. I looked at John and told him that this probably would cost us the tournament.

We had less than four minutes to get back to the check-in at Mitchell's Bay. Fortunately, we made it with about 30 seconds to spare, weighed in, and won by mere ounces. Again, we won as a result of having enough confidence to keep fishing right till we ran out of time.

John and I had another great experience fishing the SWOBA Classic on Rondeau Bay that same season. We decided to start at a breakwall that was only about 200 yards from the starting line. Because we'd had such a stellar year of fishing that circuit, winning two out of three qualifying tournaments, we were boat number one to blast off that morning. So we took off, ran about 200 yards to the spot, then stopped and began fishing.

Before the last boat went out, we had a limit of fish in the livewell. It must have just killed the other competitors who were sitting there waiting their turn to go, because this was in plain view of everyone.

The next morning they switched the starting order around, so whereas we were the first boat to go on day one, we were the last to go on day two. There were already 16 boats fishing the breakwall when John and I finally arrived. Since we had caught an easy limit of bass there on day one, we weaved right in amongst them and joined the party. We only got one fish in that pack of boats before we left, but it was the only one we saw caught there that morning. Confidence? You bet!

Nowadays with magazines, videos, books, TV, and the Internet, so-called secret techniques don't remain secret for very long, and most anglers are on a fairly even footing. All that separates first place from last place, in many cases, is the confidence that comes from being mentally prepared.

This extends beyond tournament fishing, of course. Standing on the dock of a new lake you've never fished before, having confidence that you will find and catch fish puts you in a great position to do so. Standing there thinking, "Man, I'll never find them in this much water," will not help your cause one bit.

Night Fishing

At certain times and places you can enjoy great action fishing at night. Despite the disadvantages of night fishing (hey, it's tough to see where you're casting or anything, for that matter), it can be a hot ticket to big fish.

Night fishing is definitely the way to go when it comes to catching monster walleye. As most anglers know, walleye have eyes that provide them with exceptional night vision, which is one reason why the biggest fish feed heaviest after dark. But there are other reasons too. At night you'll rarely face competition from other boats, and you'll never see a water skier or have to dodge boats racing by, stirring up the water. After the sun sets, lakes are calm and quiet, so these spooky big fish go on the prowl. In really clear lakes, big fish may feed almost exclusively at night.

Of course walleye aren't the only fish that bite well in the dark. Gary Burghoff, who used to play Radar O'Reilly on the television series *M.A.S.H.*, has been a frequent fishing companion of mine over the years, and he's a die-hard night fisherman. One of Gary's favorite pastimes is night fishing for giant smallmouth bass in Connecticut, where he has a summer house. In fact, Gary caught one smallmouth that may have been a Connecticut state record while fishing at night with a black Jitterbug.

I recall one night, fishing for giant smallmouth bass off this beach near his house. We went out there with black Jitterbugs and I caught a smallmouth that weighed over five pounds. Gary's potential record bass, which he had pulled out of the freezer at home to show me the day before, dwarfed my five-pounder.

The black Jitterbug has a unique sound to it, making it a great night fishing lure. On a steady retrieve it has this distinctive plop-plop-plop sound that really calls fish. When I fished at night with Gary we could never see our lures, but boy could we ever hear them. No wonder they work so well for those smallmouth—they're easy to find.

The black color of these Jitterbugs would seem like an odd choice for fishing in the dark, but since bass are looking up into the moonlight, just about anything they see will appear as a silhouette anyway. Color probably doesn't matter one bit. But size, profile, and sound sure do. The minnowbaits I use for those big walleye are six or seven inches long. Many anglers would say they're too big, but they're easier for walleye to find. Larger silhouettes generally work best at night.

Spinnerbaits are also good night lures, especially those with a single, large Colorado-style blade, which makes a lot of thumping vibrations. In the early years we used to go out to Buckhorn Lake in central Ontario's Kawarthas, fishing from a pontoon boat. Some friends, the

Mayberry family, would load the boat up with a number of people and throw spinnerbaits up on shallow points and shorelines of the many islands that dot Buckhorn Lake. By casting the spinnerbait out and using a medium steady retrieve, we'd catch walleye, smallmouth, and largemouth on a reasonably consistent basis. You're out there on a party boat, having fun, and catching lots of fish. Once again it was just that steady medium retrieve and the vibration of the spinnerbait that would call the fish in.

Interestingly, many of these fish were caught in one to three feet of water, in areas where you wouldn't catch them during the day. The real key was heading out after dark.

Fishing at night demands preparation. I place everything that I'll need in the open, where I can find it quickly. This includes needlenose pliers for unhooking fish, a flashlight, a landing net, and even a towel for drying hands.

It's obviously a bad idea to fish in areas you don't know well at night. I scout my spots during the day and make notes on the location of weedlines, of any hazards such as rocks or deadheads, as well as of land-marks such as cottages that I can use as a reference in the dark.

Then, once I'm out there, I try to be as quiet as possible. A heavy footfall or the banging of a tackle box lid carries a long way in the dark. You have to be extra careful and extra quiet to avoid spooking the fish.

If you are quiet though, and in the right spots, you can enjoy great action and catch some of the biggest fish of your life. Night fishing is definitely a different experience, but it can be rewarding.

One-Two Punch

For starters, no, I'm not talking about boxing here. The one-two punch is an old tournament fishing tactic that's helped me win a lot of bass tournaments over the years, as well as catch some really nice fish for the camera while taping TV show segments. It's one of those old tips that just never seems to lose its effectiveness.

Say you're fishing with another person who's using a surface lure or a buzzbait, and all of a sudden there's a big swirl as a big fish swipes at their lure and misses it. You then cast right behind that person's bait with a different lure, like a jig or a plastic worm, to try and capitalize on that fish's aggression. That's a one-two punch. If the fish chases a lure and misses, give it a quick follow-up bait and most of the time you'll catch it.

The reason I like to think of this as a one-two punch is that you're giving the fish a second opportunity to hit, but with a different bait and a different presentation. Occasionally, fish will swirl or swipe at lures

Fish that attack and miss a fast-moving lure can often be caught by quickly following up with a finesse bait, such as a tube jig. Talk about a deadly one-two punch!

and then, at the last second, change their mind. By following up with something that's slower, smaller, and more subtle, you can take advantage of the fish being all wound up, but give it something it might be more inclined to eat. This works better than simply making a second cast with the same lure.

The good news is, this is not just a bass tactic and it doesn't just have application to tournament anglers. I've used the one-two punch to catch brook trout in northern Ontario, where trout that swiped at and missed little minnowbaits subsequently ate a jig. I've also caught lake trout, northern pike, and many saltwater species by throwing a backup bait.

I can remember winning one of the early Pro Bass tournaments with my brother Wayne by using buzzbaits over a number of small, isolated weed patches and flats. Even though the fish were aggressive, and most of them were hitting the buzzbait and eating it, we did use the old one-two punch to catch a couple of very good-sized largemouth. For example, if a fish missed the buzzbait, we threw a plastic worm in the area of the swirl. The water was around five to six feet deep in most of these areas, and the fish were coming up out of the holes in the weedbed. So we were basically fan casting the buzzbaits and working the area as thoroughly as we could, but every now and then a big fish would come up and miss the bait. Then the other person, as fast as he could, would pick up a plastic worm and flip it to where the swirl was and let it drop right down into that hole in the weeds. Most of the bass were so wound up, they immediately inhaled the soft plastic worm as it settled into the openings.

Packing for a Trip

Tip 22

When you prepare for a fishing trip, it's important to take the right stuff. This sounds obvious, but you would not believe how often people arrive at a lake totally unprepared for what awaits them.

This is particularly true when you go away on vacation, especially if it's a fly-in trip and replacement tackle may not be readily available. I have been to remote fly-in camps and seen people who had just spent $4,000 to go on the trip pull out a big saltwater spinning reel with five-year-old 30-pound test on it, and a rod that doesn't match it either in weight or action. That's just silly, because no matter how good the fishing is, you will have a tough time enjoying yourself if you don't have the right gear.

When you prepare for a day of fishing, think about the type of fish you want to catch and the types of fishing you want to do. For example, if I'm going on a pike and walleye trip, I take a heavy action rod for casting big lures for pike, a medium-heavy spinning rod and a medium action baitcasting outfit for casting crankbaits of both species, as well as a medium action spinning rod with a fairly fast tip for jig fishing. Everything is targeted to the fish I want to catch, with some thought as to how I want to catch them.

When packing the essentials, think seasonally. If it's warm out, bring plenty of sunscreen and bug repellant, as well as spare clothing in case of weather changes. Never leave home without a rain suit. I always take gloves on the trips far north, even if it's the middle of the summer, because you never know when a cold front will appear. Take a handheld compass, some bandages (if you'll be catching a lot of fish your hands are sure to get cut up), needlenose pliers, and plenty of spare fishing line. If you're not taking many rods and reels with you, take a couple of clip tops for your rod in case of breakage. I like to carry a little tube of glue or duct tape as well.

Make a checklist before your trip just to make sure you don't leave anything behind. When you've traveled as much as I have and you go on trips each and every month, packing is certainly very important. If I'm not packing, I'm unpacking—every week. Even with that much practice, I still make checklists. Better that than discovering you've forgotten something important when you're miles from home.

Patterns for Success

Tip 23

If there's one trap that consistently catches anglers, it's that few practice pattern fishing.

Have you ever watched a pair of fishermen work their way along a shoreline? At almost every point, they pick up a couple of nice fish, yet they fail to realize they've discovered a pattern and continue aimlessly down the shoreline.

Obviously, what the pair should do is concentrate on the points, work each one thoroughly, and forget about the rest of the shoreline. Good patterns are hard to come by. Knowing this is often what separates the pro from the casual angler.

As soon as I get on the water, I work fairly fast, move around a fair amount, and try to locate active schools or groups of fish. I also fish as many different types of structure and cover as possible, with a variety of presentations. Whether it's fishing for the TV camera, competing in a tournament, or just fishing for fun, I never sit on one spot all day waiting for the fish to find me. I go running and gunning for them.

Onto a hot pattern? Maybe! If you catch several fish on the same bait in the same types of spots with consistency, you may have found the winning pattern of the day.

Let's say, for example, that I'm fishing with a black plastic worm and I catch a couple of bass from a particular location, say an inside turn on a weedline. Just because I've caught these fish, it doesn't mean I've hit the jackpot. But it's often the first clue to a pattern.

I then try to locate as many other inside turns on weedlines as I can find and systematically fish them with that same plastic worm. In other words, I try to duplicate the successful conditions. If I start popping bass at each spot, then I know I've found a productive pattern for that particular day.

While fishing a Pro Bass tournament in Belleville, my brother Wayne and I found fish in a number of different locations. We found shallow fish, fish on flats, fish on reeds, fish in lily beds and undercuts. It seemed we could catch fish everywhere. But we had to narrow it down to what would catch us the biggest fish out of the 150 boats in the tournament.

As we moved out of the bay, there were some isolated pencil reed patches. Some consisted of only two or three reeds sticking up in a big open expanse of water. So we tried them. We ended up catching a five-pound largemouth on one of these stands of reeds, then we caught a three-pounder. Thinking we might be onto something, we went into every bay and looked for these isolated pencil reed patches. We ended up winning the tournament with 12 bass that weighed a total of 45 pounds. Ironically, once we figured out the pattern, it was a no-brainer.

That's what pattern fishing can do for you. Pay attention to the details, and when you see a pattern forming, you're on the way to a great day of fishing.

Percentage Approaches

Tip 24

Fish are usually associated with structure and cover. But sometimes anglers accept that concept a little too religiously.

Many fishermen understand exactly what types of structure and cover to look for—it's when they find them that the real trouble begins. And the reason they often blow their chances is that they get too keen and immediately fish the best structure and the best cover.

Let's say we're fishing an ideal-looking bay. It doesn't matter what for—it could be bass, pike, trout, walleye, even muskies. As we slowly cruise into the bay though, we notice there's a weedline out in deeper water and, about halfway in, a big bed of lily pads. Way back further still, two or three big trees have fallen into the water. Now, the mistake many anglers make is that they head immediately for what appears to be the very best structure or cover. They could be right—most of the fish could be under the lily pads or beside those blown over trees. But then again, they could be wrong. Very often, the biggest fish actually suspend in open water just beside the shallow stuff, or sit on the first drop-off nearby. These anglers would be far better off if they systematically fished the deeper structure first, and worked their way progressively shallower.

I've caught thousands of fish this way, by working my way into cover rather than charging up and heading straight for it. I can remember one occasion while fishing for smallmouth bass on Lake Erie during a cold weather period. There was a really nice point I wanted to fish, but as I approached the spot, I decided to prospect the deeper water leading up to it first. So I began fishing in that 30- to 35-foot range, and immediately upon lowering down my jig, I felt a little tick, set the hook, and caught about a four-pound smallmouth. Talk about a nice start! It turned out to be an awesome day of fishing—I lost track of how many fish I caught weighing over four pounds. The largest bass weighed in at 6.34 pounds on the digital scales. If I had driven straight up to the obvious point, and not worked my way up toward it, I would have missed out on that action.

Sometimes big fish situate themselves just offshore from obvious spots. That's why you should always fish your way up to good locations, rather than drive the boat straight there. You might be surprised and catch a trophy like Justin Izumi's hawg smallmouth.

Playing the Odds

Tip 25

There's no question that playing the odds in fishing will make you a better angler. It could be fishing for giant walleye at night, it could be fishing for largemouth bass in heavy cover, it could be fishing for salmon with downriggers, or it could be fishing small jigs for crappies during the spring of the year. Successful fishing, and putting the odds in your favor, go hand in hand. Playing the odds when fishing in clear water could be using light line, which is tougher for the fish to see, but it could also be fishing during the early morning, or early evening hours, or an overcast day, when visibility is reduced. Or, if you're in clear water, go to the windward side of the river or lake. There are so many aspects to playing the odds that you have to put as many of them into play as possible to be successful.

When I won the 1990 Canadian Open Bass Tournament, I was fishing out at Main Duck Island, which is in the middle of Lake Ontario.

It's a small, isolated group of islands, mainly limestone. I can clearly remember the last day of the competition. I didn't think I could win the tournament, but I was trying to place high. Les Zacky and Bruce Leeson, two other competitors, were fishing near me in fairly shallow water, working one of several crevices that lead from the depths into shallow water. Bass follow these crevices like highways.

As the water warmed in the afternoon sunshine, the bass became more active and came out of deep water, moving into the shallows to feed. I positioned myself on a crevice on the deep side, to intercept any fish that were going to come swimming under the boat up toward them, and I proceeded to catch a number of good-sized smallmouth. I then made the long run back to Kingston and ended up winning the tournament. To this day I still say I put the odds in my favor by getting first crack at those fish.

Now don't get me wrong, because you're probably thinking that I cut Les and Bruce off. But that really wasn't the case. This is open-water fishing, and I was in deep enough water where this crack graded out into a flat bottom. But what I did was get on the highest percentage area of the structure.

Sight Fishing

Tip 26

One of my favorite ways to fish is in clear water. I enjoy the thrill of seeing the fish and tempting them into eating my offering. Over the years I've sight-fished everything from coho salmon in big water, to chinook salmon and steelhead in rivers, largemouth bass in wood and weeds, smallmouth around boulders, and pike in shallow bays. Sight fishing can be done in many clear water situations.

Ideally you should keep your body movement to a minimum. Watch your footing—a heavy step while you're in the boat will spook fish like nothing else. It's also a good idea to wear natural tones of clothing so that you don't stand out too much. Finally, you must determine which direction the fish are going. I've seen many unsuccessful attempts at sight fishing by anglers casting right where the fish are, rather than where the fish are headed. You don't want to hit the fish in the head because this will spook them.

When I won the 1994 Canadian Open bass tournament with all smallmouth bass, many of the fish I caught were in 5 to 22 feet of water. More than 90 percent of these fish were caught by sight fishing. In this case, the fish were hanging around boulders. I used soft plastic grubs and tube jigs. With the fish in deeper water, as in this case, there's always an optical illusion—the fish seem to be right below you, but they're actually farther away. The key is to cast beyond where the fish actually appear.

I love sight fishing for giant northern pike in the spring of the year, when they crowd into shallow bays. I've done this in Quebec, Ontario, Manitoba, Saskatchewan, and Alberta. I always try to cast beyond the fish and to bring the lure at a right angle toward the fish, presenting the lure in such a way that the pike's eye can pick it up more easily. Make sure you offer the bait in an enticing way to propel the fish forward. If possible, I position the boat so the fish aren't looking at me but facing away or off to the side. It's much easier to bring the bait toward the fish than to swing it off to the side. I only do the latter when I feel the fish aren't going to spook.

While sight fishing for Tasmanian brown trout, Bob had to be extra cautious to avoid spooking the fish.

In Tasmania I sight-fished for brown trout in ankle-deep water. My guide was adamant that we shuffle our feet along the bottom instead of lifting them. He said it's important not to put any rings out when walking, meaning rings on the surface of the water, or any other such commotion. If that brown trout was grazing through the shallow water, you had to determine if it was moving left or right and lead it anywhere from three to seven feet. It was some of the most exciting fishing I've experienced because it was so visual.

So, yes—I love sight fishing. It's fascinating because you get to see the reactions of the fish to your lure, positive or negative. And, like a good steak on the barbecue, sometimes the smell and the sizzle are as good as the meal itself. Anticipation is incredible!

Slack Line Set

Tip 27

Someone once told me that hook sets are free, and there's a lot of truth to this. In fact, some of the best anglers I've fished with have the habit of constantly setting the hook. Any time things didn't feel right or they saw their line move in a peculiar way, they would set the hook. Most of the time it was nothing. But every now and then—surprise!—it turned out to be a fish.

Everybody knows that the best way to set a hook is to take all the slack out of your line, and then drive your hook home hard. But this isn't always the case. In fact, one of the newest twists to hit the angling scene is the slack line hook set. And take my word for it—it's great! Wayne showed me this trick a while ago, and under the right conditions, it's the only way to set your hooks. The right conditions are almost anytime you're fishing for bony-mouthed fish such as bass, walleye, muskie, and pike with heavy lines, large hooks, high-performance graphite rods, and low-stretch monofilament lines.

Okay, now that you're rigged up properly, let's say you're out on a lake fishing and you get a good hit. Instead of quickly reeling in your line and striking when you feel the weight of the fish, leave some slack in your line. Then, snap upward with your wrists and take up the slack. In this way, you build momentum, and the power drives the hook into the fish's mouth with a sudden, sharp impact. The best way to describe what's happening is to use Wayne's analogy. He compares this method to driving a nail into a block of wood. Removing all the slack before you set the hook is similar to resting a hammer on the head of a nail and then trying to push the nail into the wood. But in the slack line method, you create momentum and power before impact, just as a carpenter does when he draws his hammer back before driving in a nail.

When you use this method you'll actually hear your line swish as it cuts through the water and air. Next time you're out after heavy fish with powerful equipment, try the slack line hook set. You'll be hooked!

Surface Strikes

I've said this before, but no matter whether you're fly fishing an Adam's Dry for trout, or twitching a Rebel Minnow for smallmouth bass, taking one fish off the surface is usually more exciting than catching a whole bunch underneath. But, while it's one thing to draw a fish up to your surface fly or lure, it's something else again to actually hook it.

I'll never forget filming in the early years of my TV show with my sister-in-law, Jocelyne, for northern pike on the Cree River in Northern Saskatchewan. Here we are in pike heaven—there are pike everywhere in the shallow weedy bays. Jocelyne, for what it's worth, is in great physical shape and has incredible reflexes.

So we're fishing these shallow-water pike using Heddon Moss Boss surface spoons, casting them along weed edges, working them over open holes in the weeds, or occasionally tossing them right into the thick stuff. Because they're just coming off the spawn and are super-aggressive, the pike are cruising around in as little as six inches of water, chasing minnows about like sharks. They're coming from 20 to 30 feet away to eat our lures—you cast and then there's this huge V on the surface as a pike slashes through the shallows to plaster the Moss Boss.

Jocelyne probably missed her first 20 strikes because she tried to set the hook too quickly. As soon as she saw the pike inhale her bait, she reacted and, more often than not, pulled the lure away from the fish. To her detriment, she was faster than some of the fish.

If you don't give fish at least three seconds to take the bait, chances are you won't catch them. Even though you can see the strike, you have to make sure you feel it first. I admit this is much easier said than done, especially when you have pike eating your lure on every cast. But waiting till you feel the fish before setting the hook will result in your hooking more fish that eat surface presentations.

That's true even when you're using lures like a Zara Spook, or a Heddon Pop-R, which have two needle-sharp treble hooks.

Fly fishermen used to use a simple system to allow trout time to take their dry flies before setting the hook. As soon as they saw the hit, they would mumble "God Save the Queen!" under their breath. It sounds silly, but the words bought them enough time to hook the fish more often than not.

Over the years I've fished with many people—all have had different ways of allowing fish enough time to turn away with a surface lure. Some closed their eyes and waited until they felt something, others slowly reeled up any slack line, while still others bit their lower lip. Do whatever works for you.

The point is though, if you haul back when you see the strike, most of the time you'll miss the fish. It doesn't matter how you do it, but waiting till you feel the fish—before setting the hook—is the key to getting those fish into the boat.

Jocelyne Izumi proudly shows off one of the big Cree River northerns that didn't get away.

Teaching Kids How to Fish

Tip 29

I'm a lucky guy in that I host a television fishing show for a living. I get to fish some of the best spots in the world, with some of the best guides and best anglers on earth. Occasionally I get to fish with celebrities, such as actor Gary Burghoff, hockey legend Darryl Sittler, or major-league pitcher Pat Hentgen. Yet through it all, my biggest thrills have come from fishing with my kids.

Teaching your children how to fish is the best investment you can make in their well-being. Fishing teaches kids patience, it teaches them about the value of life, it teaches them the importance of wilderness and a clean environment, and I think it teaches them a lot of values and responsibilities that carry through to everyday life. Most kids have a natural curiosity about the natural world, so chances are they'll jump at the chance to go fishing. Even if that's not the case, once they're out in the sunshine it's hard not to have a good time.

The most important thing to consider when you teach your kids to fish, especially at first, is that the day is really their day—not yours. So don't push them. If they get bored and decide they want to go catch frogs instead, then go catch frogs. Forcing them to fish when they've grown tired of it will only turn them away from fishing, perhaps for good.

Fishing has to compete with many things for your children's interest, so do things that keep it visually stimulating and fun. Fish for anything that will bite—perch, sunfish, crappies, and chubs are great. Choose fishing that has lots of action. Big fish aren't nearly as important as lots of fish. And go at it simply, with worms or minnows at first. Just playing with the worms or watching a bucketful of minnows swim around is great fun for younger anglers. When you catch a fish, put it in the bucket so they can watch it swim around.

Kids are the best fishing partners you could ever ask for!

When I fish with children, I like to fish with a sensitive little float. Kids love watching it go under when they get a bite (me too!) and it keeps things visually stimulating.

It's also important to bring along plenty of snacks and drinks. We adults tend to overlook how quickly children can become thirsty or hungry.

Some of the best conversations you'll ever share with your children will come when you're in the boat or on the bank of some little pond or stream, fishing. In the outdoors they can relax and enjoy themselves without the distractions of the phone, cartoons, the Internet, or video games. While fishing you have their undivided attention.

I like to take my son on at least one major trip, like a fly-in trip, every year. When Darren was 11 years old he joined me on a trip to Knee Lake, in northern Manitoba, which is known worldwide for its tremendous pike and walleye fishing. We got into an area of the lake where the pike were going absolutely nuts on the surface. They were blowing up everywhere, chasing minnows. In all my years of pike fishing I'd never seen activity like this. So we rigged up with topwater lures. I figured Darren would have a great time watching the pike explode on his lure, and I have to tell you, I was every bit as excited as he was. We had a blast.

Darren and I were both using a Sputter Buzz, which is a surface bait with a propeller such as you would find on a buzzbait. Since we were also taping a segment for my television show at the time, and I wanted to promote the lure for my sponsor, I asked Darren, rhetorically, if he had any room in his tackle box for it. He looked at me and with the

50

most apologetic face you could imagine said, "Nope, I like it, but my tackle box is full. I don't have any room for it." Talk about a classic moment.

At the end of that trip, I asked Darren what he thought, and he said, "Dad, this is the best." At that moment, all the years of baiting his hooks, pouring his drinks, and untangling his tangles suddenly seemed worth it.

To Stay or to Go

There's no question that making the right decisions when you're on the water can pay off with lots of fish. Perhaps the biggest decision you can make is how long to stay and fish a given spot.

This question is loaded, because how long you should fish an area depends on how big the area is, how deep the water is, how clear the water is, and what technique you are using. I don't want to confuse you, but there's no simple answer to this question, apart from saying that everybody's comfort level—when you feel you've exhausted an area either by catching fish or not catching fish—is different.

One of my tournament competitors, who's very successful, always fishes his spots methodically and thoroughly. His approach is the opposite of mine—I fish a number of areas quickly and put more miles on the boat than he does. We both do well despite the fact that our approaches are poles apart. If you ask each of us how long to fish a spot, you'll get two very different answers. It's impossible to say that one of us is right and the other wrong.

I can remember running into him during practice at one tournament. He was fishing a bay that was about five to eight acres in size. I went to the same bay and fished for about an hour, caught a couple of fish, and then left. I went on to fish five other spots, and hours later when I drove by the bay, he was still there!

So how do you determine how long to fish a given spot?

I think you have to consider your strengths in fishing. If you're really good at certain techniques, for instance, ones that cover a lot of water, then you're better off to run and gun and cover a lot of water. For example, if you enjoy fishing with buzzbaits or crankbaits or spinnerbaits, techniques that cover vast amounts of water in a short period of time, you're probably going to be more successful fishing several spots quickly, and fishing a number of spots over the course of a day. You'll probably be happier, and more successful, if you move more often.

But if you're an angler who enjoys fishing slowly with jigs or plastic worms, carefully picking the cover apart with slow-moving baits, then you're better off fishing in this way because this is your strength. You will be happier and more successful fishing spots longer and more carefully, giving them more time before moving on to new locations.

That said, there are times when staying and fishing hard, or leaving and trying new spots, will make the difference regardless of your personal preference. The decision to stay or go comes down to your knowledge of the lake. If you know the fish are there, sometimes it's better to stay and wait them out.

In one tournament a few years ago, I was fishing a spot with about five boats on it. They all came, stayed for a few hours, then left, because the fishing was tough. I stayed the whole time and caught four big fish—big bass that enabled me to win the tournament. I got my four big bass because I was stubborn and decided to stay. I knew when I got a bite that it was a big fish, even though there were few fish in the area. Being stubborn paid off in this case.

The opposite can be true in situations where you don't know if the fish are there or not. That's when you're often better off to go looking for them.

So whether you stay or go depends on your own strengths and weaknesses, as well as your knowledge of the lake. Weather can also play a hand.

When the conditions are good and the fish are active, it's almost always better to do the miles. This is when you can pull up to a spot, catch a couple of fish quickly, then, when the action dies down, go somewhere else and again appeal to active fish. I've observed this when bass fishing in tournaments, as well as when fun fishing for walleye, pike, muskie, and steelhead.

But when conditions are tough, such as when there's a lot of angling pressure, boat traffic, or inclement weather, it's often better to stick around, fishing much more slowly and thoroughly, really working the spot completely before thinking of moving on.

Trolling Techniques

Tip 31

No doubt about it, trolling is one of the best fishing techniques for covering water and locating scattered fish. But it's important to realize trolling is more than simply throwing lures behind the boat and going for a drive.

Trolling is a way of covering expansive areas quickly and efficiently, rather than just wandering about aimlessly. Have a game plan. Decide which areas are most likely to hold fish and work them in a systematic way, so you cover all possible angles and approaches. If you suspect walleye are suspended off a point, for example, be sure to try both sides of the point, and to experiment at different depths and distances from the point itself.

Trolling speed is an important consideration, especially if two or more anglers are fishing from the same boat. Not all lures are created equal in terms of the speed that gives them the best action. For example, let's say you and I are trolling from the same boat. I'm using a flutter spoon; you're using a crankbait. Chances are that if we troll slowly enough for my flutter spoon to work properly, we'll be too slow for your crankbait. So when trolling, it's important to ensure that all lures used will operate at the same speed.

Some lures have a narrow range of speeds that give them the best action, while others perform well over a broader range of speeds. With time and experimentation, you'll learn how each of the lures in your tackle box works best.

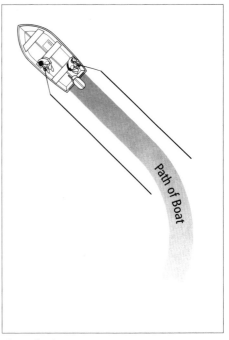

The lure on the outside of a turn (right) will work faster than the lure on the inside of a turn (left). If you catch more fish on turns, that's your cue to adjust your trolling speed accordingly.

I like to set the boat speed, then physically check each lure before letting line out, especially if we're downrigger fishing or in any other situation where we have numerous lines out.

Modern Global Positioning System (GPS) units will display your exact trolling speed through satellite technology. They offer the ultimate in accuracy and eliminate the fear of getting false readings from wind or current. If you're catching fish at 1.7 miles per hour, it's a good idea to take note of the lure you're using. If the combination of speed and lure is producing fish, you should continue at that speed.

One common mistake, particularly when downrigger trolling with several people in a boat, happens when one rod or lure seems to get more hits than the others. Thinking that there's something different about that one magical lure that's getting all the bites, most people will immediately remove the lure they were using and rummage through their tackle box trying to find a bait that's the same color as the one getting the hits. Color *is* important, but it's also critical to select a lure that works best at the same trolling speed. Simply switching to a similarly colored lure will do you no good at all unless your new selection develops peak action at the same speed as the one catching all the fish.

Another common mistake, particularly when trolling across a lake and not catching a lot, occurs when you decide to take a swing back to where you started. Then, on that turn, you get a strike or a fish. This happens because when you turn the boat, lures on the outside of the turn automatically begin moving faster, while those on the inside edge slow down. If you keep getting hits when you turn the boat, this should tip you off that you need to adjust your trolling speed up or down a notch. Try trolling in a zigzag pattern instead of going straight, and see if there's any consistency to your bites. If you're always getting bitten on the outside rod when making a turn, that's your cue to speed up.

Varying Your Retrieve

If fishermen aren't careful, they can develop a number of bad habits that eventually cost them, both in action and in fish. One of the easiest habits to develop is to not vary the speed of your retrieve. If you stick with the same style and speed throughout the entire fishing season, you're going to miss out on some great action.

I came to appreciate this many years ago when fishing a bass tournament on Lake Magog, which lies on the Quebec-Vermont border. It was an early season bass tournament, so there were still a number of smallmouth to be found in very shallow water. I was using a Bomber Long A, jerking and ripping it through the shallows. I saw a smallmouth bass and a big shadow behind it. I decided to speed up the bait because I only had about 10 feet of line left before it would be on my rod tip. A fish had been following for who knows how long, yet the moment I sped up, it rocketed forward and ate the lure. As a result I landed my biggest smallmouth of the day. This incident was an eye-opener, and from then on, I became more aware of my retrieve speed.

On the other hand, sometimes it pays to go more slowly than you normally would. When the surface of a lake is calm and the fish are in relatively shallow water, I love to cast a floating minnowbait, such as a Rebel Redfin, and let it lie totally motionless on the surface until the rings have disappeared. Then I'll twitch it ever so gently, so that it barely moves at all. This retrieve can only be described as excruciatingly slow. However, if there are bass around, they'll usually wallop the daylights out of it.

There are other times when you'll want to retrieve your lure just as fast as you can crank the reel. Burning a Cordell Spot along a weedline, for instance, is a favorite method of mine for triggering strikes from aggressive fish. It's amazing sometimes just how fast you need to crank that lure in order to attract the fish.

Varying your retrieve also makes sense when you're fishing earlier or later in the year. Fish are cold-blooded creatures, so their activity levels are directly related to the water temperature. So when fishing during cold weather, you'll often find it's best to slow down a bit.

The opposite is true in midsummer, when it's 90 degrees in the shade and fish metabolism is at its peak. That's when you can have great success fishing fast. Fish that ignore traditional offerings may respond to your lure just because it's going so fast. It appears different from the other baits they've grown accustomed to seeing. And don't kid yourself for a moment about going too fast. If a fish wants your lure, you can't reel quickly enough to pull it away.

This applies to trolling as well as to casting. Slow down in cold weather, speed up when it's warmer. I have a friend who trolls for rainbow trout in the Great Lakes during midsummer, running the boat at six to eight miles per hour. He hammers fish, too. Considering almost everyone else goes from one to three miles per hour, he's not only making his lures appear different, he's also covering more ground over the course of a day, showing his lures to that many more fish.

My strangest trolling speed experience occurred when fishing off the coast of British Columbia in Whale Channel, trolling cut baits for the late run of fall coho salmon. I looked down beside the boat and, lo and behold, a coho was swimming beside the boat. I couldn't believe it. I quickly reeled up my bait, plopped it down beside the boat, and swung it around so that it was in front of the salmon. Nothing. I swung the rod again, speeding up the bait, and the coho drilled it. Did speed make a difference? I believe it did.

Wading

Tip 33

It's amazing to think that after producing over 300 episodes of the *Real Fishing Show*, the most talked-about shows have been the ones where I've been wading for northern pike. No question, wading is a fun way to fish. It's also extremely effective.

Wading works for a couple of reasons. First, it's dead quiet. You don't have to contend with the typical boat sounds, like feet banging on the floor, tackle boxes scraping across the deck, or the hum of the electric motor. Nor do you need to worry about the wind blowing you out of position or into the cover. You're low in the water, so fish are less likely to be frightened by your shadow. And, if you move quietly enough, they'll accept the sight of your legs as just another drifting log.

Wading is a great way to get close to fish, whether it's working a shallow weedbed for pike or largemouth bass, fishing a river for trout, salmon, or channel catfish, or casting spoons off shoreline points and creek mouths for lake trout and walleye. I'm always amazed at just how close to the fish you can get. Over many years of shooting underwater footage for my TV series, numerous cameramen have been able to walk right up to fish I would never have been able to approach in the boat.

Wading is fun because it's just you and the fish, toe to toe. This can make for some really interesting experiences.

For example, a few years ago I was fishing a shallow, weedy bay by myself using a big Heddon Zara Spook. There were some huge pike in

Wading works, whether it's for bass and pike in a pond near home, or for Arctic grayling in the Yukon.

this bay and I was having a ball catching them. At one point, this big old pike came out of nowhere and ate the lure very close to where I was standing. As it ate it, I hoped that it wouldn't run toward me and crash into my legs. Sure enough, it came at me like a torpedo, and the only thing I could think of was the Zara's treble hooks getting caught on my privates. Luckily, I lifted my leg just in time—the pike zoomed by and didn't get caught on me.

On another occasion, fishing at northern Manitoba's legendary Knee Lake with my friend Bruce MacDougall, we scouted the area first in an aluminum boat. We found a school of three or four large pike in a spot with about four feet of water. Perfect! We parked the boat in the shallows, hopped over the side, and waded out toward where we saw these fish. We caught every one we spotted.

We used a quick video clip of one of those pike in the opening of my TV show for a couple of years. In the clip Bruce is fighting a really nice pike when all of a sudden it launches out of the water and comes sailing right toward me. Afraid that it's going to spear me in the head, I throw up my arms in self-defense and turn away—thankfully, it crashes back into the water and swims off.

Kamikaze pike aside, wading is also quite safe, provided you observe a couple of simple rules. Don't go too deep, don't get overly adventurous in stained or off-colored water where you can't see the bottom, and try to stick to hard bottoms like sand or rock for easier going. Watch for current areas, and always be extra cautious in those situations. Bringing along an old ski pole to use as a staff for more leverage is always a good idea, as is wearing a Personal Flotation Device (PFD)— just in case.

Once you get comfortable in waders, you'll find that wading can be addictive. Being one-on-one with big fish in shallow water may be some of the most exciting fishing you'll ever experience. And some of the most productive too.

CHAPTER 2

Where to Fish Tips

Backwater Fishing

Tip 34

Some days it seems there are more boats on the water than fish below the surface. When this happens, it's time to throw your boat and motor into the back of your pickup, and head for some out-of-the-way, backwater fishing holes.

Most often, the big lakes and rivers get all the press. Yet some of the best fishing, whether you live in British Columbia, central Canada, or the southern States, is tucked away in small lakes, ponds, and rivers. And, because most of these spots have no formal launching ramps, or rough gravel ones at best, they're ideally suited to small boats that can easily be carried down to the water and that will handle most weather conditions.

Canoes are ideal for fishing in many of these small spots, as are small 12-foot aluminum cartoppers and plastic boats such as the Coleman Crawdad. Small waters seldom have big waves, even when the wind howls full force. This alone makes them great spots to fish on days when you might not be able to get onto bigger waters due to inclement weather. You can bring along a small outboard, like my favorite little six-horsepower Merc, or simply go with an electric motor. My little 12-pound thrust MotorGuide pushes a small boat around all day on a single battery. It's also very helpful for simply positioning the boat.

A number of years ago, when fishing in south-central Florida in the irrigation waters that surrounded an orange plantation, we realized we didn't have an electric motor for our small boat. We decided one of us would have to get out and drag the boat around while the other got to fish. Fortunately for me, Wayne lost the coin toss and he got to wade around in the alligator-filled water, dragging me around as I cast to all of the likely looking cover. We ended up having a blast catching largemouth bass in these ponds and canals.

Don't for a second believe that small lakes are only capable of growing small fish. While it's true that some remote back lakes are overloaded with stunted bass or other species, just as many have monster fish that never see lures. I caught one of my biggest brook trout ever from a tiny little pond way back in the boonies, while fishing with pro guide Frank Clark, who used to live in Elliot Lake, Ontario. It was a lot of work getting into this little lake he knew, but he assured me that once we got there, we'd have a great chance of catching a trophy brook trout. He was right—I got one just a hair under six pounds.

I've also enjoyed some incredible back lake fishing for warm-water species, including largemouth bass. On one occasion, former Toronto Blue Jays pitcher Pat Hentgen and I clawed our way into a deserted little back lake I knew in central Ontario and had a great time catching decent largemouth bass. The greatest part was having the lake all to ourselves.

So when the crowds get a bit much, remember there *is* an alternative. It takes a little more work, but the rewards of back lake fishing can be well worth it.

Spot on a Spot

Tip 35

I could go on and on about spots; this is something we've pushed for 20 years now in our educational seminars. Essentially, a spot is the premier location of fish on structure, break lines, shorelines, weedlines or weedbeds, even boat docks. For example, some spots on docks are much better than others; a preferred spot for fish is the location where the motor is always started and stopped and digs out a little hole.

The question is, How do you find these spots? The best way of finding the real honey hole, the spot where you pull up and your first cast results in a fish, usually requires groundwork on the water. On occasion, I have covered an area 300 to 400 yards long, such as a large shoal, for an hour or so before throwing my first cast. What I'm looking for is a spot on that large shoal that distinguishes it from the rest of the shoal. It could be a flat bottom that all of a sudden has a rock pile three or four feet in diameter; it could be a fairly steady drop, or break line with a wall or underwater bluff. On Lake Simcoe, there are precise areas that we'll go to for smallmouth bass, and if you're 20 to 30 feet in the wrong direction either way, you're out of luck. You're not going to catch fish unless you get right on the spot.

In New Brunswick, in one of the early bass tournaments on Lake Mactaquac, where I had limited time to practice, I looked for a pattern more than for specific spots. In this case what I found turned out to be

Finding a shoal that holds fish is always a good thing. Finding which end of the reef the fish are concentrated in is even better—this is finding the spot on the spot, and it's your ticket to big catches, both on open water and through the ice.

both a pattern and a spot on a spot. The lake is a large, man-made reservoir, and I was basically looking for something different. As it turned out, if you looked at the rolling farm fields that came down to the bank, every now and then you could see a fence row that would come down through the pasture. Along a number of these fence rows there were feeder creeks. Many of these creeks were trickling into the lake. I found that I could catch one or two smallmouth at each of these stops along the shoreline. The area I fished had probably at most an 80-yard circumference. Back in those days there were not many weeds on that lake, but I found an isolated cabbage weed patch along one shore that also held some good smallmouth. Because it was along a nothing-looking shoreline, this weedbed was certainly significant.

In a similar fashion, at a tournament on Lake St. Clair, we were fishing along a fairly standard sandbar for smallmouth bass, but there were isolated dark patches that stood out. With polarized sunglasses you could see these dark spots, and by using big spinnerbaits and long casts, we ripped the spinnerbait over them. All of a sudden these big smallmouth appeared out of nowhere. The cool thing was that this was a visual spot that you could see simply with your glasses, unlike a spot on a spot where you need your electronics to see, such as a sharp break on a drop-off, a rock pile, or a crevice. These visual spots were certainly productive.

Tip 36

Fishing Fallen Trees

Once you have a certain amount of fishing experience, you begin to recognize certain clues as to the likely whereabouts of fish. One of my favorite clues is a big old tree that has fallen into the water. Fallen trees can be cover for trout, bass, pike, and muskies—in fact, just about every species of fish.

The best fallen trees sit with their branches covering a drop-off—the tip of each tree in much deeper water than its base. Trees also need some lead-in cover or structure as well—some sort of route the fish can follow to and from them. Isolated trees sitting in shallow, empty water aren't nearly as productive as big old trees that wind up on the deep side of a major drop-off, or in the deeper end of a weedbed.

In bass tournament fishing, it's amazing how anglers often overlook the shallowest trees. Even the shallowest trees, as long as they have adequate lead-in cover, will hold bass on some of our lakes. Sometimes they can be the best because they get the least amount of fishing pressure.

Regardless of where they're located, the important point to remember is that fish beside fallen trees are usually ambush predators. This means they're not roaming around the area, but they're tucked up under the branches waiting to catch something to eat.

Fishing fallen trees therefore calls for precise and accurate casting. The fish usually won't move far for your lure, so it's got to be right on the mark. The best approach is to carefully fish around the farthest submerged portions of the tree first. Work your spinnerbait, worm, tube, jig, or crankbait into every little nook and cranny.

Only when you've carefully fished the point of the tree should you start to move back down the sides. And then you should do it systematically. Make several casts parallel to the tree, and tick the branch ends that are lying off to the sides. Once you've done that, start slowly working down one side of the tree and then the other, carefully looking for pockets between branches where you can flip or pitch lures.

Fallen trees can hold a number of species of fish: bass, walleye, muskie, pike, channel catfish, crappies, perch, or trout. Exactly which lures to use depends mainly on where you're fishing and what it is you're trying to catch.

Fallen trees form terrific cover for a variety of species.

Not many anglers think of fallen trees as trout cover, but this is often the case. I recall one fishing trip to north-central Ontario's Elliot Lake for brook trout, on a small back lake that I'd never fished before. First we went around the circumference of the lake with the electric and noted several fallen trees. We ended up catching a number of brookies by doing nothing more than pitching small jigs into these trees, starting with the deepest part of the tree, and letting the jig sink down to the bottom. If we didn't catch anything right away, we would work our way along the tree, winding up right beside the trunk and lowering our jigs down into the shadows beneath it. Those trees made for a great day's fishing.

Fishing from Shore

Tip 37

Many of us started out fishing from shore as kids. And we learned plenty from this experience to make us better anglers as we grew older.

But this doesn't mean shore fishing is just kid stuff. On the contrary, there are times and places where you can catch far more fish from the shore than you can from the boat. Sometimes it's the best approach of all.

For example, I remember growing up on Rondeau Bay, where we would shore fish the canals for crappie. We'd use small floats and a foot or two of line with a small jig or minnow. As the season progressed and bass fishing opened up, I remember fishing anything that looked bassy that I could reach with a cast from shore. There were times I'd be driving around the bay and see a log in the water. I'd stop, grab a spinnerbait, throw it along the shady side of the log, and catch a big bass. Many times we'd walk several miles of shoreline. One of our favorite areas was an old junkyard. We'd catch bass that were sitting in the junk. In fact, one old submerged refrigerator always seemed to have a bass in it. We'd also fish the pier where we'd catch perch and sheepshead, and the moss-covered wood pilings where we'd catch bass.

Even now there are times when I'll pull the boat up against the shore and intentionally fish from land. In fact, a mistake many anglers make is assuming that the grass is always greener on the other side of the fence. Or, in this case, in the middle of the lake. On most lakes, a large number of the fish are tucked right in on the shorelines.

The key to fishing from the shore is to pay attention and to be observant. Look for spots where large trees have fallen into the water and for weedbeds, rock piles, and boulders close enough for you to land a cast. And fish around docks, rock cribs, and even swimming platforms. Breakwalls form a great edge that can hold decent numbers of fish.

Regardless of your fishing hole though, pay particular attention to its shaded side. And when you're walking on a dock or along the shoreline, move quietly so you don't spook any nearby fish.

Also, never start by casting out to the farthest spot. Remember, fish can be hiding anywhere alongside the type of cover I've mentioned. So work your way out gradually, and drop your lure into every potential fish-holding pocket and crevice.

Can't catch fish without a boat? Not true. We've been doing it for years and having fun along the way.

Fishing Muddy Waters

Tip 38

It may seem ironic, but a famous blues singer also happens to be one of my favorite fishing conditions: Muddy Waters!

In fact, no matter how you describe such conditions—dingy, dirty, stained, off-colored, or muddy—they are all ideal for fishing. That's because fish that live in crystal clear water usually have a keen sense of sight. Because of this, they can detect even minor flaws in your presentation.

It's a different story when fish inhabit dingy water conditions, such as you find off creek mouths following a good rain, or along wind-swept shorelines after high waves have stirred up debris. Under these conditions fish are more apt to rely on their sense of smell and hearing to home in on prey.

You can take advantage of their reduced vision by using lures that vibrate and produce plenty of noise in the water. Because the fish can't see well, they tend to become reflex feeders, striking out at anything that crosses their paths. Lures such as the Cordell Spot, which have bearings that rattle built into them, can be deadly under these types of conditions.

For the steelheader, taking advantage of off-colored water might mean using hot pink mesh to tie up a roe bag—not very natural-looking, but certainly very visible in dingy water.

Many years ago I went on a trip to New Brunswick's Miramichi River to fish for Atlantic salmon. Heavy rain caused the river to swell up over the banks. I was fishing with legendary fishing guide Vince Swayze. We fished a number of areas along the river and caught quite a few fish, even though the river was much higher and muddier than normal. I credit this to Vince, who knew where the salmon would position themselves in such a high water situation—in spots which would be shallow under normal conditions. He also used big flashy flies that the fish could easily see.

When fishing in off-color water, it's important to slow down and give fish an opportunity to locate your offering. Fishing in water that is shallower than normal can also help you get more hits.

On another occasion, catfishing in Manitoba, the same thing happened—lots of rain, lots of high water. Yet we caught fish by switching to spots that were shallower than the guides would ordinarily fish. Muddy water will put fish shallow for a number of reasons. When the water has color, they don't need to be down as deep, and there's a whole flush of new food with the rain.

Even though it might look bad, off-colored, muddy water can offer great fishing. Under these conditions expect fish to move a bit shallower than normal, and use brighter, noisier lures. You might be surprised with the results.

Fishing the Blue Lines

Tip 39

Years ago, Joe Hughes, who works for Pradco, a company that manufactures lures, introduced me to a terrific way of finding overlooked fishing spots. Basically, you pull out your road map and take note of all the little blue lines or creeks on it, especially the ones that cross under roads, the kind you see over the course of a country drive. These are creeks that, for the most part, seldom get fished. On a day's drive you can try a number of these places. Believe me, you wouldn't believe the fish we've caught in some of these nondescript creeks that meander through the countryside.

Fish often hide under roads, under the shade of a bridge, or even in fully closed-in culverts. These spots can hold everything from brook trout, rainbow trout, brown trout, smallmouth bass, and largemouth bass, to pike, muskies, crappies, and other panfish. There's no question that these spots hold fish, yet many anglers overlook them. I guess they seem too obvious or accessible.

Rick Matusiak, who shoots a lot of underwater footage for my TV series, is a master at fishing the blue lines. A number of his dynamic underwater shots have been videotaped in the shadow of the highway. The way he looks at it, why hike for miles when there's plenty of fish right at the road?

The key is to match your tackle to the location. At most of these little blue lines or creeks the water is clear, so it's a good idea to go with light line (four- or six-pound test) with smaller presentations. I can remember seeing a video of Joe and Lisa Hughes fishing in one of these small creeks in the US. On the video, they catch a nearly eight-pound bass on a tiny crankbait. In this regard, some of the most productive artificial lures I've used over the years have been a series of minibaits such as the Rebel Crickhopper and the Rebel Crawfish, as well as the small Cotton Cordell Big O. These small, ultralight crankbaits look so natural the fish can't resist them.

Fishing with Lake Maps

An accurate map of a lake's bottom can be as important to your fishing success as your boat and motor or rod and reel. Unfortunately though, not all lake maps are created equal. In fact, some are much better than others.

The ones I like best include contour lines. I find these maps preferable to maps that show only specific spot depths. The contour lines connect all of the areas on the bottom that have the same depth, so when you look at one of these maps, you get an accurate picture of just what the lake looks like under all that water.

After I spread out a map for the first time, I try to locate all the potential fish-holding structures. I look especially for those areas where the contour lines run closely together. These spots identify quick drop-offs.

Alternatively, I zero in on areas where the contour lines are far apart, and where the water is fairly shallow. These spots often represent feeding flats over which fish love to roam.

Some lake maps even provide symbols that tell you whether the bottom of the lake is sand, rock, or mud. And the very best maps go one step further—they show you the location of reeds and weedbeds.

What do you do if there aren't any maps available of your pet lake? Well, you still don't have to fish the lake blindly. You can find plenty of clues from the surrounding shorelines.

What you find on shore is often strikingly similar to what lies beneath the surface. Say, for instance, the shoreline is flat and marshy. This normally indicates that the adjacent lake bottom is also flat, and probably soft, shallow, and weedy. I repeat this visual procedure for the whole shoreline, whether it's steep and rocky or moderately sloping and sandy. This shoreline check gives me vital clues as to the nature of the lake bottom.

If a lake's not too large, I give it a quick once-over, checking all of the lake's shoreline features. Sometimes, I'll speed troll with lures trailing behind our boats, but most often, I'll just run the lake with the motor wide open. I take note of structures such as underwater points, bars, saddles, and humps, as well as cover such as weeds, reeds, boulders, and stumps. Once I have a good mental picture of the lake, I'll start fishing each of the preferred spots quickly.

A contour map is a valuable aid, but if one is not available, don't get discouraged. Often these mysterious, uncharted waters are the very best—especially when you know how to go about unlocking their secrets.

Sonar, used in conjunction with navigation charts, can help you locate hidden reefs, shoals, saddles, and other fish-holding structures that many anglers miss. Whether he's fishing a tournament or just out for fun, Andrew Klopak always uses charts to his advantage.

Knowing Lake Types

Tip 41

If someone told me that tomorrow I was going to fish an oligotrophic lake, I could right now, sight unseen, describe that waterbody and the fishing conditions to a tee.

Because there are so many lakes in the world, scientists have devised a way to describe and compare them. They use a simple system of three broad groupings. A lake is either oligotrophic, mesotrophic, or eutrophic. Now, those are pretty fancy sounding names; yet, the common word in each is "trophic." What trophic means essentially is fertility. So, lakes are simply classified according to their richness and

productivity. Oligotrophic lakes, for example, are nutrient poor; while mesotrophic lakes are moderately fertile. The real granddaddies, though, are the eutrophic lakes. They're super rich and productive.

Oligotrophic lakes (upper right) are typically cold, deep, and infertile. Eutrophic lakes (upper left) are the opposite of oligotrophic lakes—shallow, warm, and nutrient-rich. Mesotrophic lakes (lower left) represent the midway point between these two extremes.

The neat thing about knowing what type of lake you're going to be fishing is that you can visualize what it will look like and where the fish will be found. You can get a good idea, for instance, if the lake bottom will be rough and rocky, or flat and muddy. And, you can predict whether the water will be shallow or super deep. You can even guess maximum and average depths.

There's even more. You can gauge whether there will be thick weedbeds or none at all; even whether the water will be cloudy or clear. And, what's most amazing, you can predict the kinds of fish that will be found in the lake, simply by knowing what type it is.

Back in the 1980s, I was hired by an old-time fishing club that had been around since the 1800s to do a crash course on catching various species of fish using different techniques. This club bordered a very large bay off of Georgian Bay. Looking at this lake I quickly identified it as an oligotrophic lake; it was nutrient poor, deep, and clean. To find lake trout I searched out deep break lines that would attract them in their search for food. For bass and muskie, any patch of weeds in the infertile water would be a fish magnet, so I looked for weeds and rock rubble near shoreline structure. I didn't know the lake, but I used my previous knowledge of other oligotrophic lakes to find the fish quickly. The moral of this story is, depending on the type of species and lake you're fishing, you should use different techniques and fish different depths and types of cover and structure in order to catch those fish.

Locating and Fishing Points

Most fishermen know that bass, pike, muskies, and trout often hide behind some form of cover, such as cabbage weeds, lily pads, boulders, or fallen trees. They hide in these areas waiting to ambush prey. But just knowing this fact isn't enough to help you. How you present your bait or lure to these fish is what determines the winner.

Points may mark places where geologic features such as faults or eskers enter the lake. These features can provide great structure for fish.

One of the biggest mistakes we see anglers make is casting right into the spot where they think a big fish is hiding. They notice an old tree stump with just its head poking above the water on a flat, for instance, and then drop a lure right beside that piece of wood. If there were a fish beside that stump though, the noisy, splashy overhead entry of the lure would surely spook it. So, a preferable presentation would be to cast well beyond that stump, then retrieve your lure so it passes by where you think a fish is hiding. This way the fish has a better opportunity to spot your lure as it approaches.

One of the reasons points are so good is for ambushing. On many new bodies of water, I run and gun and fish as many different types of points as I can, trying to figure out what the fish are holding on, in what depth, and in what type of cover structure. In many cases you can be fishing points, but unless you're on the exact spot of that point, you're not going to get fish.

In the early years of walleye tournament fishing, back in the late '70s, I remember fishing one prominent point on southern Ontario's Lake Scugog where my brother Wayne and I were catching a few scattered fish, but the guys in the boat beside us were just walloping the fish. They were nailing them left and right and ended up winning the tournament. After the tournament it was driving me crazy that 30 feet from us they were catching so many big walleyes. I asked one guy, "What were you guys doing?" And he said it wasn't so much what they were doing—we were all using jigs—but where they were. They were sitting on a submerged tree on a point, and the walleyes were in this tree that was no bigger than their boat. So they were lowering down and spanking these big walleyes.

Points are great places to contact fish. Those with a bit of depth nearby, and with good structure, can be big fish gold mines.

Another technique that I use occasionally in bass tournaments is to run around and fish nothing but wind-blown points with big spinner-baits. Keep in mind that when you have wave action on these points, there might be some (in this case) largemouth in the weedline that might come out of the weeds and start working along the edges of the rocks and become more active on these exposed points. On a lake such as Rideau Lake there are some islands where, under windy conditions, you can catch a couple of big fish by running and gunning spinnerbaits.

Tip 43 •

Looking for Edges

One question I'm asked repeatedly is where to find fish. And I always give the same answer, whether the person fishes lakes, rivers, streams, or the ocean. The quickest way to locate fish is to look for edges.

So what's an edge? Put simply, an edge is where two different types of habitat meet. And it's the diversity that edges provide that makes them so attractive to fish. The two most obvious edges in a lake are right at the surface, where the water runs into air, and right at the bottom, where the water runs into rock.

And while this sounds simple, these two edges can be super fishing spots. At certain times of the year, fish seem secure when they can relate to the bottom. Species such as walleye, bass, and trout spend a good deal of time actually resting down there. At other times of the year, they'll relate almost exclusively to the surface.

Fly fishermen, for instance, dream of being on a river when a mayfly, caddis fly, or stone fly hatch is underway and the surface is packed with rising trout. Bass fishermen usually think they've died and gone to heaven when the fish are hitting surface poppers and floating stick baits.

Slightly less obvious edges to be on the lookout for are ones that rim cover, such as fallen trees and exposed boulders. Other edges include those that border weed, reed, and lily pad beds. These edges are often great spots because fish can hide in the shadows and pick off minnows that wander out into the open or come in to hide along the edge.

Even spots that at first glance appear featureless, such as riprap banks, have edges, if you look carefully. The areas where large boulders meet smaller rocks is one example.

One of my all-time favorite subtle edges is the one that's created where light penetration ceases and total darkness begins. Fish love to hide just under that massive shadow and feed on overhead baitfish that are silhouetted against the surface. To determine the depth at which this edge occurs, simply tie a white cup to a piece of line, and ease it over the side of your boat until you lose sight of it. Then, measure the depth at which you lost sight of the cup and double it. That's it. If you lose sight of the cup at 7 feet, the so-called twilight zone edge is at 14 feet. The reason for doubling the depth is simple—it accounts for the fact that light has to penetrate down to the object and then bounce back up to your eyes. In the fish's world, light penetration is a one-way street. So if there's enough light to reflect off a white cup at 7 feet, there's enough left to see at 14.

Another subtle edge that fishermen often miss, and believe me, it's one of the best, is when the bottom of a lake changes from one type of material to another, say from soft muck to hard gravel. On many occasions, there's no change of depth involved, but the bottom composition definitely switches. Unless you're paying close attention, you're going to miss these transition areas. But to the fish, they're as noticeable as neon signs.

A depth sounder is the easiest way to find these transition areas, because your signal will be much stronger as soon as you cross onto the harder bottom. And if you have a gray line feature on your unit, you'll see the band expand or contract, depending on its hardness. I continually check what's underneath me, especially when I'm fishing in water where I can't see anything with my polarized sunglasses or when I'm fishing deep water. Sometimes, a depth change as subtle as six inches can make all the difference in the world.

All these theories about the importance of edges have been proven, thanks to the proliferation of underwater cameras. When you lower these cameras into the depths of lakes and rivers, you can see fish relating to transitions, from sand to rock, from a hard bottom to a soft bottom, or from a weed edge to no weeds. To see it in black and white (or in living color) is truly amazing.

Structure Fishing

Tip 44

One of the most important fishing concepts, and one we often take for granted, is structure. Fishermen talk about structure as though it were a religion. They even refer to themselves proudly as structure fishermen.

Actually, the term structure was coined by American fishing pioneer Buck Perry, almost 30 years ago. Buck so revolutionized fishing with his concept of structure, that he's recognized today as the grandfather of structure fishing. Probably the best way to describe what structure is, and to explain how Buck changed our way of fishing, is by example.

Back in the 1940s and 1950s, most anglers fished only the shoreline of a lake, or the visible cover, such as reeds and weeds, things they could see with their eyes. But Buck showed them that there were plenty of big fish in deeper water, fish that were associated with distinct changes in the bottom of the lake. He called these changes "structure." This is the best and easiest way to remember what structure is—it's any change in the bottom of a lake. It might be a huge, rocky underwater point, a ridge, a saddle that connects two islands together, a sunken reef, or a hump. These are all changes to the bottom of a lake, so they're all types of structure. But most important of all, they're all fish magnets, and this is why you should be concerned with them.

Back in 1981, I was with fellow tournament angler Hank Gibson, on our way to Manitoba for a fishing tournament. We decided on the way to stop in at Nestor Falls, Ontario, on Lake of the Woods. We'd never been there before and didn't have any navigational charts of the lake. We only fished there the one day, but we caught a number of smallmouth bass and walleye on this piece of structure we found. Not knowing where any of the reefs were (Lake of the Woods is notorious for its shoals), we stuck fairly close to the buoy markers. We happened upon one marker that was obviously signaling there was something there, so we idled up to it and found it marked a shoal. We ended up catching a number of decent-sized smallmouth bass on top of the shoal in about 10 to 15 feet of water. As we dropped down and fished our jigs slowly around the deeper part of the shoal, we caught a number of walleyes in 20-plus feet of water. Two species of fish on the same structure, just at different depths. That day taught me that structure will hold several species of fish, although they may be located at different depths.

We continued on our way to the tournament, arriving in Manitoba the next day. The organizers had a boat arranged for Hank and one for my brother Wayne. I was fishing with a brand-new Ranger. Once again, navigational charts weren't available, so neither of us had any idea where the reefs and shoals might be. As it was a walleye tournament, this was important information. Since I had never fished this area before, I decided my strategy would be to get away from the crowd on my first day on the water. My idea was to run maybe 20 miles down the lake and look for areas the other groups weren't fishing. I was running a 150-horsepower Mercury then. I ran down the lake at full throttle and all of a sudden I saw this dark spot. There was no way I could stop or turn, and being from southern Ontario, I prayed that it was nothing more than a thick offshore weedbed. In the south it would have been a safe bet that it was weeds, but this far north you might be wiser to put your money on something of a slightly harder substance. Guess the odds weren't in my favor; it was granite. I was going so fast the impact sheared the skeg off of my lower unit. With a bent prop shaft and no skeg for steering it made an interesting trip back to the tournament headquarters.

On the positive side, I did find a great shoal. Now let me tell you, I don't recommend this method of locating structure. I've found a hydrographic navigation chart and a fish finder both work just as well, and are a lot less expensive.

Structure versus Cover

If you spend time around fishermen, you'll discover they have a language all their own. In fact, it's often so individual that a word can mean something to one fisherman and something totally different to another. Let's take the important concepts of "structure" and "cover" as two good examples. And boy, are they ever important. That's why it's critical to clear up the confusion that surrounds these two terms.

I define "structure" as any change to the actual bottom of a lake or river. A good illustration of this would be if we were slowly trolling along a flat, featureless shoreline and then came upon an underwater point that ran out several hundred feet into the main lake. Since that point is a distinct change in the bottom of the lake, it's a form of structure. And the same thing would apply if the bottom change was caused by a sunken reef, a large shallow shelf, or an underwater saddle that joined a couple of islands together. Since these things are all changes to the bottom of the lake, they're known as structure.

Structure describes bottom features such as rocks, drop-offs, and shoals.

"Cover," on the other hand, is something that is usually found *on* or *on top of* the bottom. A bed of cabbage or coontail weeds, for example, isn't structure, it's cover. The same thing applies to flooded timber and submerged trees. They're both cover as well. Structure is any change to the bottom of the lake, while cover is something on that bottom.

It's important to define these terms properly because once you understand their exact meaning, you're well on your way to uncovering some real fishing hot spots. Because, as good as structure and cover can be on their own, put the two elements together in the same place, and you just might find a honey hole you're not prepared to share with anyone else.

If you want to know what cover can do, take a school of emerald shiner minnows and dump a couple dozen of these into a tank or bucket and then throw a rock inside. It's incredible how the fish will come over to the rock as if it were a magnet and hang around it. Well, this is how cover can work, or how something unusual on a piece of structure can work.

Cover refers to things found on top of structure, such as weeds and logs.

I can remember fishing with John Vandivier on Lake Erie at a bass tournament in the early years. We were fishing on a sandbar for largemouth bass, and the sandbar was pretty vacant of cover except for this small weed patch with a stump in it. The water was crystal clear, and when we spotted the stump, we saw a school of fish swimming around it. There were a number of largemouth, one smallmouth, and a few panfish using this stump as cover, and they were holding to it along the sandbar, which was obviously structure. It was like driving along a highway and all of a sudden seeing a coffee shop. We backed up with the electric motor on low so we wouldn't spook the fish, and we proceeded to catch every fish. I think there were about seven or eight fish there, and I remember having a small tackle box for what I call finesse baits for sight fishing. We took every one of those fish off that piece of structure by rotating various pieces of plastic (little reapers) using split shot rigs, small hooks, and six-pound test line. We kept the biggest ones and ended up winning the tournament by weighing in some of the fish that we caught off this stump. Ideally, it was a key area along the sandbar that saved our bacon in that tournament.

CHAPTER 3

Boating Tips

All About Downriggers

Tip 46

Not long ago, if you wanted to fish in deep water, you basically had two options. You could add a ton of lead, or else you could troll with wire or lead core lines. Diving planers, which look like a little disk or triangle, and which attach to your line a few feet up from the lure, also work to get deep. But when you need precise depth control, it's pretty tough to beat a downrigger.

A downrigger resembles a winch clamped to the back or gunnel of the boat. The downrigger reel is spooled with heavy braided wire, which is held away the boat by a short boom arm of two to four feet in length. On the end of the cable, there's a 10- or 12-pound lead ball with a fin on it (called a cannonball). Either on the ball itself, or attached to the cable just immediately above it, is a clothespin-type device called a line release. How it works is simple—you just play your lure out behind the boat, then clip your line into the line release. Put your rod in a holder, and look at your fish finder. If it says the fish are 57 feet down, you watch the depth counter on the downrigger as you lower the ball, taking your line and lure with it. When it hits 57 feet, you know your lure is right on the fish's noses.

Next, you wind up the slack line, so your rod is in a cocked-over position. When a fish hits, the rod will either spring up (which happens when the fish hits and comes toward the boat), start bucking wildly (when the fish stays put and shakes its head), or slam down and the reel will scream out line (when the fish goes the other way). Either way, you grab the rod and the fight's on.

In addition to allowing you to troll with incredible depth precision, downriggers allow you to catch big, deep-water fish without having any clumsy weights on your line. You could even use an ultralight rod and reel if you like, or even a fly rod. There's no need for heavy action outfits and wire lines.

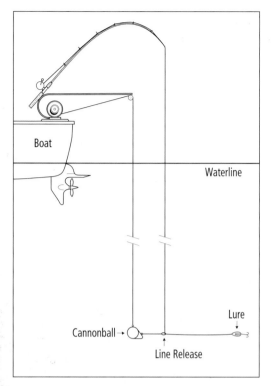

Boat

Waterline

Lure

Cannonball →

Line Release

Downriggers allow you to troll a lure with precise depth control. When a fish hits the lure, the line releases from the down-rigger weight and you fight the fish with no extra weight or drag on your line. Trolling with the rod cranked over in a tight arc helps recover slack line after the strike and provides a visual ref-erence for spotting hits. When the rod flies up or begins to bounce, fish on!

Downriggers make it very easy to follow drop-offs and different depth contours. As you work your way up or down a drop-off, you can let out or take in cable as required to keep your bait right above the bottom. When lake trout are in a sleepy mood and not interested in chasing lures, dragging the cannonballs along the bottom and stirring up the sediment can really wake them up. Or on lakes with wildly erratic, granite bottoms, you can raise and lower your bait to avoid getting snagged up all the time.

Downriggers are immensely popular with salmon fishermen, who rely on them to work schools of baitfish in open water. Their simplicity makes them ideal for novice anglers or kids, or even for advanced fishermen who just want a relaxing day. My son Darren is becoming addicted to this method of open water salmon angling. Not long ago he caught his first-ever chinook salmon on Lake Ontario off St. Catharines, trolling with downriggers. The rod popped up in the holder, Darren grabbed the rod, and a big king salmon, that later weighed in at about 28 pounds, took off for the far end of the lake. Darren's eyes opened as wide as I have ever seen them, and all he could do was hold on. It was like he had hooked a truck—the fish was screaming away and there was nothing he could do to stop it. At one point he wanted me to take over, but it was his fish and I refused. I'll never forget how relieved he looked when the fish finally went into the net.

Downriggers can be installed in any type of boat. John Vandivier, one of my tournament fishing friends, even has a set installed on his Ranger bass boat. He has a mounting plate for his two riggers that plugs into the rear pedestal hole of his boat.

Downriggers are not just for salmon and lake trout fishing. Many people use them for walleye, muskies, or even deep smallmouth bass. I was introduced to one of the strangest ways of fishing with downriggers several years ago on the Niagara River. Even below the falls, as the river flows past the giant Adam Beck power plant, the Niagara is a big river with a wild current. Most people fish it by casting from shore, or drifting from a boat, using their electric motor to make necessary course corrections. But a small number of anglers have discovered a unique use for downriggers. They anchor their boat, and use the down-riggers to keep their lures working near the bottom in 25 to 35 feet of water. The swift current provides all the action the lures need. Any passing salmon gobble them up and the fight's on. I'm sure, as time goes by, people will figure out even more unusual ways of using downriggers. Think whatever you like, they *do* work, and that's tough to argue with.

Anchoring Tricks

• Tip 47

Last spring, with guide Dean Roy, I fished on Red River in downtown Winnipeg—right in the heart of the city amongst tall apartment buildings. We had anchored and caught a few catfish in this one spot. Dean then wanted to move to a new location, so I started to pull the anchor up. One problem—it wouldn't move.

I bent my knees, kept my back straight, and hauled hard on the rope. It gave only slightly, and I had to ask Dean for help. I hadn't paid attention to the anchor when he dropped it, but now I was wondering just how big it was. It felt like we were pulling up another boat. We both hauled on the rope, and with a lot of work, we got the anchor up to the surface. I couldn't help laughing out loud —the anchor had snagged a tire, one of the flukes had gone right through the center of the rim. To this day, I believe Dean should have kept it, because it had more tread than some of the tires on his truck.

Many times over the course of a fishing season, you will want the precise and accurate boat control that only anchoring can give. Yet many fishermen have trouble with their anchors. Either they drag along the bottom and fail to catch, or worse yet, they get so badly snagged, anglers wind up having to cut the rope. Even though I normally use my electric motor to position the boat, I've learned a lot about anchoring, and like anything else, there are tricks to it that make life easier.

For starters, unless the area you're fishing is super calm, you shouldn't really tie your rope directly to the anchor. Instead, attach a short piece of heavy chain, about two to four feet long, to the anchor. And then tie your rope to the chain. The benefit of the chain is that it acts like a shock absorber while your boat is anchored in rough water. When a wave lifts up the front of your boat, the chain absorbs most of the energy. So there's less direct pull on the anchor itself and less chance it'll drag along the bottom. A simple thing, but it works like magic. Try it.

Then, there's the importance of letting out the proper length of anchor rope. In boating terms, the amount of anchor rope is called the

If you fish mainly on calm lakes, you can simply tie your anchor directly to your anchor rope. But if you often fish in rough water, use two to four feet of heavy chain between the rope and the anchor. The chain acts as a shock absorber, preventing the anchor from tearing free, and lessening stress on the boat.

scope. And the standard rule-of-thumb ratio is four to one. So, if you're fishing in 10 feet of water, put out about 40 feet of line. If you're fishing in snaggy waters, or using an expensive anchor you don't want to lose, tie a second line between the flukes of your anchor. This way if you get stuck pulling on the main rope, you can back your anchor out by tugging on the secondary line.

The invasion of zebra mussels in the Great Lakes has led to much discussion about the positive and negative effects on our fisheries. If you talk to walleye anglers they'll say it's negative, but the people who fish for smallmouth say it's been positive. One positive thing has been the increase in water clarity. With my polarized sunglasses on, I've found three anchors, two rods and reels, another fishing reel, and countless lures stuck on the bottom. It's kind of like treasure hunting. My collection of anchors continues to grow.

Battery Care

Batteries supply the energy required to power our motors, lights, livewells, flashers, graphs, and Global Positioning System navigation systems. They're often ignored, yet they're the heart of any fishing boat. Don't believe me? Well think again, because if anything goes wrong with your batteries while you're on the water, your fishing is going to suffer.

Car batteries won't cut it in a boat—you need marine-grade, deep-cycle batteries for items such as downriggers and electric motors, as well as a good marine-grade cranking battery for your outboard motor. Marine batteries are built extra-tough, to handle the stress of trailering and fishing in rough water.

I've been to numerous fishing tournaments, with big money on the line, and watched anglers slip in the standings for no other reason than their batteries failed to deliver. Fortunately for you, this doesn't have to happen, provided you maintain them properly. This means keeping the battery posts clean and free of corrosion. Regularly pop off the battery caps to check the fluid level—make sure it's where it should be. Distilled water is the best stuff for topping up batteries; I keep a jug of it in the garage, next to my battery chargers, for this purpose.

Speaking of chargers, it's important to keep your batteries fully charged. Not halfway there or three-quarters charged, but topped right up. This will result in longer battery life and a lower tendency to develop charge memory. Some chargers can be permanently installed in the boat. Not only are they shockproof, but they're waterproof as well. When it's time to charge your batteries, simply plug them into an extension cord and you're in business. Make sure they are unplugged before you head out. Many fellow pro anglers have been in a hurry and forgotten to unplug their chargers. Knock on wood, it hasn't happened to me...yet!

While it's important to maintain your batteries during the fishing season, it's doubly important to check on them during the winter, when they're sitting idle. Make a point of inspecting them every few weeks and, if necessary, putting them on charge overnight. If you follow a regular maintenance schedule, come spring your batteries will be fully charged and ready to go fishing—just like you.

Caring for Your Outboard

I'd be rich if I had a dollar for every fisherman who is going to jump into his boat this spring, turn the key, and hear his motor groan. After a long winter of anticipation, this is super-frustrating. Especially when there is no reason for it to happen in the first place. But whether your motor starts in the spring or not really depends on how well you stored it the previous fall. Despite what some people think, sitting out there under a pile of snow all winter can take its toll on an outboard motor. So, an ounce of prevention in the fall is worth a pound of cure in the spring. But that's water under the bridge if it's already spring. If that's the case, you have work to do.

The first thing to do is change the oil in the lower unit. Most outboards have a pair of screw holes on the side of the lower unit casing for this purpose. Drain the old oil, then pump in new lower unit oil from the bottom. Be sure to completely fill it until the oil begins to ooze out the top hole. Make sure that you replace the small gasket on both screw plugs. Put the upper plug in first to create a vacuum. The lower plug has a small magnet, which collects any loose gear filings from the lower unit. Make sure it's clean before you insert it.

It's also a good idea to fill the gas tank and add a fuel stabilizer if you're going to store the boat for a long time. Filling the tank eliminates the possibility of condensation forming, which would contaminate the fuel, and might foul the engine. According to Mercury Marine Service, fuel can go bad in as short a time as three months. They recommend QuickSilver Fuel Stabilizer to prevent fuel breakdown in storage.

Last fall, while storing some of our company boats, I found a problem on one of our Lund aluminum boats. This particular boat has a 40-horse tiller on it, and it had been used by a number of people during the season. I took out the screw plugs on the lower unit to check the oil and discovered this creamy-colored water and oil ooze, indicating that water was getting into the motor somehow. I immediately got it to a Mercury dealership and they replaced all the lower unit seals.

I always make it a point to change the spark plugs every year as well. New plugs virtually guarantee a season of easy starts, optimum gas mileage, and smooth trolling—and they only cost a few bucks. They're one of the best investments you can make.

Last but not least, take a grease gun and give a few good squirts everywhere you see a grease fitting. Also give the motor a quick visual inspection, particularly the area around the propeller. Make certain no fishing line or dead vegetation is fouling up the motor, under the prop or elsewhere. You might want to give the motor a quick wash to freshen its appearance too. That will help protect its finish and keep it looking new for years. Modern outboard motors are incredibly trouble-free. But taking a few minutes to keep them clean and well-serviced can extend the motor's life, and reduce the chances of a problem on the water.

Electric Trolling Motor Batteries

Tip 50

In my high performance or tournament boats I use a three-battery, 36-volt system. Some of today's more powerful trolling motors, such as the MotorGuide Tour Edition, which has 107 pounds plus of thrust, require a three-battery setup. By using a 36-volt trolling motor, I find that running it on 36 volts, so that you're drawing down three batteries instead of two, gives you a much longer time without having to recharge. Same for my smaller boats, which use 24-volt motors powered by two batteries. They last much longer than the older 12-volt, single-battery versions.

The key is amperage. Without making a big deal of it, the greater the voltage, the lower the amperage draw. Any battery has only so much power (measured in amp hours). Reducing the amperage draw will result in longer battery life between charges.

One thing I would recommend is top quality, deep-cycle batteries. I use both Group 27 and Group 31 electric trolling motor batteries. These are big suckers, with much more oomph than the standard Group 24 batteries most anglers buy. Nothing is worse than running out of power before you're finished fishing. Although the big cells cost a bit more, they're worth it in reliability and overall life, because you're not drawing them down as much.

For the most part, it's important to keep your batteries fully charged. I'll never forget in the early '80s how I'd gotten busy and dropped my boat off at a compound to store for a few months after a winter Florida trip. I didn't top the batteries up. About a month later I returned. It had been an extremely cold winter that year, and I opened up the battery compartment and one of the batteries had actually frozen, expanded, and blown up. Because it was discharged, the acid wasn't active and moving. Talk about a mess. Remember that if you leave a deep-cycle battery drained for any amount of time, chances are it won't recharge or be as efficient.

One of the most popular options with modern fishing boats is a built-in battery charger. I highly recommend them. When you come back from your trip, to your hotel or to your home, just plug them in and you're all set. These are shockproof, waterproof, built-in chargers that don't cost much more than regular chargers but are certainly much less hassle.

One final tip, especially if you're staying at a hotel and not at home—make sure the circuit you plug in to actually has power. This sounds obvious, but it's amazing how easy it is to overlook this detail. A friend of mine plugged his battery charger into the plug in the hotel room, went out for dinner, then hit the sack. Next morning, expecting to find his batteries completely charged, he was shocked to find they were only at 25 per cent capacity. The next evening he figured out the problem—when he went to sleep and turned out the lights, he was also turning off the power on the receptacle he was plugged into. It was a switched receptacle. Plugging the charger into another outlet solved the problem, but not taking the time to check cost him time on the water.

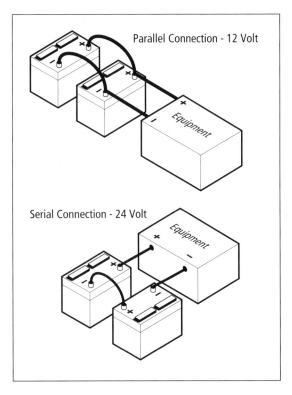

How do you wire two 12-volt deep-cycle batteries together? A parallel connection will result in a 12-volt power supply with essentially twice the running time. A serial connection, on the other hand, delivers 24 volts.

Fuel Saving Tips

Tip 51

Few things in life are certain, except death, taxes, and the rising cost of boat gas. For this reason, people are becoming more and more interested in learning how to improve their boat's fuel economy.

The best way to reduce fuel consumption is to slow down. Not too many fishermen realize it, but by simply reducing the speed of your boat from full to two-thirds throttle, you can save up to 50 per cent in gas costs. Over a full season of fishing, that's a substantial amount of money.

Balancing the weight inside your boat is another important consideration. Always try to distribute passengers and gear so that your boat can easily get up on step and not plow in the water. Once it is planed out, trim your motor so as little as possible of the boat is actually in contact with the water. By reducing drag this way, you'll shave more savings off your fuel bill.

Keeping your motor properly tuned is another good idea. Not changing your spark plugs each year may save you a couple of bucks in the short term, but in the long run, it'll cost you more in poor fuel economy.

Even the simple act of keeping the bottom of your boat free from algae will pay big dividends. If you trailer your boat, dry it with a chamois each time you take it out of the water. And, if you keep it permanently moored at the marina or at the cottage, spend a few minutes on a warm, sunny day and scrub the hull with a soft bristle brush.

If you have an older motor, you might consider replacing it with a newer one. Modern outboards are incredibly fuel-efficient. If you fish often, you'll notice huge savings—more than enough to justify the purchase price. For example, the new Mercury Optimax 225-horsepower outboard uses at least a third less gas than my old 200-horsepower outboard used to. In fact, it uses almost 40 per cent less fuel. Direct fuel injection and computer technology make these motors state-of-the-art. They are also far more reliable, and virtually smoke-free. The new generation of four-stroke outboards are also much easier on fuel and oil than older outboards, while running cleaner besides. Mercury's Optimax and four-stroke outboards are much better for the environment.

Saving a few bucks here and there adds up. By thinking about what you can do to reduce your boat's fuel consumption, you can probably save enough each year for a new rod and reel, a fish finder or Global Positioning System, or even a trip south in the winter months. Now there's incentive!

Getting There Safely

Tip 52

As I was driving down the Niagara Escarpment a number of years ago, doing about 50 miles an hour, I suddenly hit one of those bumps in the road. Things did not feel right. I looked behind me, and swaying five feet on either side of the truck is my Ranger bass boat. The hitch had come loose and the only thing holding the Ranger to my truck was the safety chains. Luckily there was nobody beside me because the boat was snaking back and forth behind me. I slowed down at the foot of the hill and carefully pulled over to the side of the road. To my amazement, the damage was minimal—I had bent the bumper on my Suburban, and the trailer's dolly wheel post was bent from sliding under the truck. One of the two safety chains had also broken right off. To this day I still can't believe I didn't lose the whole rig.

I suspect what happened was that when the person who had just cleaned my boat hooked it up to the trailer, the hitch coupler wasn't seated correctly on the ball. The coupler wound up sitting on top of the ball, rather than down and around it. Since neither of us had checked, it was only a matter of time till it popped free.

When towing any sort of trailer, you have to make sure your trailer coupling device is adjusted properly, especially if it's new, so that it will fit your ball correctly. Most couplers have a spring-loaded nut underneath; you push up and turn a nut to adjust the pressure of a spring that holds it in place. If you don't take the time to make this adjustment, you run the risk of having the hitch pop off the ball one day and, believe me, that's not as much fun as it sounds.

Taking the time to check and, if necessary, adjust your trailer connections will ensure that you make it to the lake and come home safely each and every time.

Proper trailering requires paying attention to details such as these. Most of us have seen trailers on the side of the highway, with one of the wheels off. This usually indicates that one of the trailer bearings has blown. It could be that a seal on the bearings is gone and the grease has leaked out, or that water has gotten into the bearings and done them in. On all my boat trailers I get the bearings checked at least once a year. That's very important, especially if you do a lot of mileage with a trailer in tow.

Getting there safely also means adjusting your driving style when towing a trailer. Make sure you always take your corners wider than you normally would, so you don't clip the curb. Having your tires properly inflated is also important. If you notice irregular tire wear, it could indicate a balancing problem or that one of the wheels (or even the entire axle) could be out of line. Better have it checked.

I also strongly recommend you have brakes installed on your trailer, whether they are a surge type or electric. Keep in mind that when you're trying to slow down for a traffic light or a stop sign, a big trailer is added weight, and it will push your tow vehicle. Brakes help immensely, but you still have to allow more stopping room any time you trailer. That's especially true when driving in wet conditions.

I recall one rainy day when one of my ex-cameramen was coming off the expressway. As he approached the first corner at a normal driving speed, he started to go into a skid. The truck and trailer jackknifed—thankfully no one was hurt and there was minimal damage to the truck—but he ruined a $3,500 boat trailer. This accident could have been prevented simply by driving more slowly than normal.

Proper Boat Launching

Tip 53

If you want great entertainment on any given weekend, take a lawn chair and a cooler of refreshments, and set up beside your local boat ramp. It can be absolutely hilarious watching people launching and loading their boats. I've seen people slide or fall into the water, vehicles back into the water, and boats sink. I've seen props get chewed up because someone trimmed the motor and didn't realize there was only 10 inches of water there when they fired up the motor (which, incidentally, I don't think is a good way to sharpen the blades). I've seen people gun it when loading or launching and, as a result, send their partner flying into the water. The possibilities for mishaps are endless.

One of my most embarrassing moments unloading the boat came

Easy in, easy out.

this past fall on a bass-fishing shoot. We were going to tape a bass-fishing segment, and I'd just hired a new assistant. I'd only worked with him for a day or two, and this was the first time we had launched a boat together.

When you remove the straps securing the back of the boat to the trailer, it is customary to remove both straps at the same time—one from each side of the boat. My new assistant (who shall remain nameless) only removed the strap from "his" side of the boat. I saw him with a strap and assumed he had removed them both.

So it looks like we're ready to go and I'm in the boat, being backed into the lake. The boat is a brand spanking new 22-foot Ranger bass boat, and I'm proud as I can be to be seen in it. I mean, this is the Cadillac of bass boats. There was a construction crew nearby working on the pier and watching us launch the big Ranger—maybe 20 guys who were my audience as I fired up the 225-horsepower Mercury and put the motor in reverse to back off the trailer.

Of course, the boat didn't budge. This is a new boat to me, so I'm there waving for the crew to back up even farther in the water while I'm hammering the gas, almost in full reverse, and going nowhere. Then, all of a sudden, the bow of the boat floats up and begins to spin around to one side. The stern, on the other hand, remains anchored in place. The trailer is much heavier than the boat is buoyant, and it's actually starting to bring me down. I must have looked like a huge fiberglass bobber being tugged at by some giant fish. By this time, I'm starting to lose it.

I told them to stop backing up, put the motor in neutral, and reached below the water as far as I could in an attempt to determine what on earth was wrong. That's when I felt the tie-down strap, still attached to the boat. I couldn't believe it. Luckily one of the construction workers, who was wearing waders, came over and helped us out. We had to push the nose back on the trailer, as it was sitting sideways on the trailer by now, then drive it out of the water, remove the strap, then do the whole thing over again. I'm certain the construction guys must have laughed about it all afternoon. I was dying of embarrassment.

My assistant later confessed that he took the strap off "his" side of the boat, and simply assumed I would take the strap off "my" side. My reply at the time was, and I still stick to it, if you take one of the transom straps off, you take *both* off. If you do anything at the rear of the boat you do it all, not just part of it. If you put the boat plug in, or take the transom straps off, or the motor support off, you do it all—not just your side of the boat. That said, it was partly my fault, too, because I assumed he had taken care of both straps. Never assume. Actually, it's always good policy to do a quick circle check before launching—walk around the boat and ensure everything's as it should be. Then you can rest assured you'll never be the one having problems at the boat ramp.

Rough Water Boat Handling

Tip 54

Have you ever been up to your crotch in cold lake water, sitting in the boat, completely dazed and confused? If not, consider yourself lucky. I have, and it's usually been the result of spearing a wave.

Spearing a wave is something all tournament anglers dread. If you fish big water and you're in a high performance boat, sooner or later you'll make the wrong decision and catch a wave just so. It's going to come over the front of the boat and, depending on how much water you catch, it's going to feel as if somebody has taken a huge 50-gallon drum of water and thrown it on you from two or three stories up. It can certainly knock the wind out of you. I've heard stories of windshields being broken and of Global Positioning Systems and fish finders being blown right out of their mounts. It's always a hair-raising experience. Quite frankly, this has happened to me only when driving too fast for the conditions.

Even if you never fish tournaments or head out on big water, it's still a good idea to learn a bit about rough water boat handling. Each year people drown in boating accidents that could have been prevented.

First of all, it's important that your boat be loaded properly at all times, but especially when you have to negotiate rough water. Obviously you don't want too much weight in the front of the boat when you're in big waves. Instead, make sure the weight distribution is focused more toward the middle and back of the boat. This will keep the bow higher, so that you don't spear any waves.

Power trim and tilt can be your best friends when operating in tough conditions. Constantly, throughout the tournament season, I see guys bouncing down a lake in their high performance bass boat with the power trim and tilt cranked up as if they were running 70 miles an hour, but they're only running 40 miles an hour. They're just banging

the heck out of their passenger and their equipment. In a chop you want to trim your motor in, so that it uses the V bottom of your boat to cut the waves. But don't trim it in too far, or you'll drive the bow down and risk spearing a wave. If you're in waves that have some distance between them, such as when you're going up and down into the swell, you might have to trim your motor up slightly so that you keep the bow up as you come off the crest of the waves.

There's no question that when you are either going with waves or against them, it can be difficult to maneuver the boat. Going straight into the waves will slow you down and give you and your boat a pounding, so rather than take big waves head-on, I usually take them at an angle or quarter into them.

Every angler should make a point of learning proper techniques for driving boats in rough water. While it's always best to avoid dangerous situations altogether, you never know when weather conditions could change without warning. Being prepared to deal with wild weather just makes sense.

Quartering may put on more distance, but I'll still get there faster than someone taking the waves straight on.

It really is true that the driver of the boat takes less of a pounding than the passenger. If you're a passenger in rough water, make sure you've got both hands on either a handle or an area you can hold onto securely. And use your legs as shock absorbers. I've seen guys in rough water just sitting there with no weight on their feet, and they're bouncing up and down like a basketball in a NBA playoff game. Keep your feet firmly planted on the floor and take the weight off of your rear end. You'll have a much easier ride this way.

If I'm in super rough water I'll wear two rain suits—one inside the other—as well as a proper-fitting Personal Flotation Device. It's hard to be happy when you're cold and soaking wet.

In a Pro-Am tournament at Belleville, Ontario, a couple of years ago, I decided to gamble and chose to fish a great spot on the New York side of Lake Ontario. The problem was, it was more than 100 miles away. So each day of the tournament, I drove my boat across Lake Ontario to my spot, fished for about two hours, then spent the rest of the day driving back. Of course, right in time for the tournament, the wind came up—hard. I'll never forget that tournament, running in my Ranger with a 225-horsepower Mercury on the back, driving hours and hours through six-foot waves. But in the end, the gamble paid off and I won the tournament. Today, I'm not sure which is the stronger memory—winning the tournament or driving more than 400 miles through six-foot waves over a two-day period.

Another rough water memory involves a tournament on Mitchell's Bay, on the northeast corner of Lake St. Clair, while fishing with my good friend John Vandivier. John and I wanted to get away from the crowd, so we ran from Mitchell's Bay across Lake St. Clair, down the length of the Detroit River, and into Lake Erie. That left us about an hour and a half to fish before we had to pack up and head back. We squeaked out a top 10 finish and, if I'm not mistaken, won $150 in prize money. It didn't quite cover the $135 a day in gas we burned over the two-day tournament, but I still think it was worth it. I'll never forget arguing with John on the way to the tournament site on the second morning. I wanted to go back to Lake Erie again, and he was ready to kill me because of the sore body he'd had from the first day of running.

The worst part about the long trip was returning in the afternoon through the Detroit River. The river is full of boats, and I mean everything from little fishing rigs to cigarette boats to Great Lakes freighters. They all leave these big wakes that bounce off both the Detroit or Windsor breakwalls. The breakwalls don't dissipate waves; they just bounce them right back. So there are waves and wakes going through that river that you can't read. I swear we were out of the water more than we were in it. I do remember the batteries being ripped out of their holders by the end of the trip. No wonder John was upset.

Although you may never have the inclination to fish in tournaments or make long drives through rough water, it's still worth knowing about rough water boat handling. Sooner or later, all anglers will have to face some big waves. A little knowledge can make your experience more comfortable, or possibly even save your life.

Subtleties of Using Electric Motors

Tip 55

Electric trolling motors have come a long way in recent years. In the mid-1970s when we used electrics, we powered them with old car batteries and felt lucky if we got three or four hours use out of them. The motors themselves were fairly weak compared to today's (my newest MotorGuide generates more than 100 pounds of thrust), and not as reliable. But they were quiet and they did allow you to keep your boat in the best position to catch fish. So despite their faults in the early years, electrics were critical tools for all anglers.

As an example of how far things have come, let's back up to southern Ontario in 1977 when I was fishing the Rondeau Bay Bass Tournament with my partner, George McTavish, in this little 15-foot bass boat with an 85-horse motor. It was my first real bass boat. George and I were fishing against each other in the same boat. It was a strange arrangement. On the first day of the two-day tournament, we fished together as a team and won by throwing spinnerbaits up into shallow bushes and catching largemouth bass. But on the second day things changed to an individual format, and we fished against each other. Because of a lack of boats in the event, we even brought a third guy on board our boat, so now there were three of us all competing against one another.

Because it was windy, we started fishing the calm side of the bay. All three of us were catching fish. I had the most—five bass I believe— while George had one, and the other guy I think had one as well. Then we decided to try the south shore of the bay, where we would work a spot we called the old stone house, basically a flooded stone foundation that had some good waves blowing onto it.

The wind was blowing out of the north, pushing the boat right into the structure. I had to turn the boat and hold the bow in place with the electric motor, facing right into the wind while trying to stand up and not fall out of the boat. That was a chore in itself—to actually fish the spot, I had to cast over my shoulder along the whole length of the boat past the two other guys.

Of course, George began cranking in fish like crazy, as did our other companion. George, in fact, filled out his limit on that spot, and ultimately won the tournament, while the third fellow, whose name escapes me, wound up catching the biggest bass of the day. I wound up having to settle for second or third place, and the knowledge that at least I was a good guide that day. The lesson to be learned is that, without an electric motor, I wouldn't have been able to hold them in position so they could weigh in their catches.

Today's electric motors are far more powerful than the one I used on Rondeau Bay, and they're powered by proper deep-cycle marine batteries that deliver much more energy than you could ever get out of an old car battery. If there's one tool that will help you catch more fish, it's an electric motor.

The simplest electrics are the transom type, which just clamp onto the back of the boat. You can get them in a range of power ratings, and with all kinds of different features. If you're a walleye fisherman and you like to back troll, they're the answer. Most models will allow you to reverse the control head so you can back troll in forward gear, giving you more thrust and battery life.

Bow-mount motors, which attach to the front of the boat with a folding bracket, come with the option of hand or foot control. Foot-control models leave both hands free for fishing, while hand-control give you more deck room, since there's no pedal and cable to eat up space.

Regardless of which kind you decide on, electric motors make it easy to keep your boat positioned in just the right spot so you can fish more effectively. They're also quiet, so you can work through the shallows without alarming fish or letting them know you're there.

When using my electric motor, I like to keep on the lower settings as much as possible. Not only does this greatly extend your battery life, but it also allows the motor to operate much more quietly. This is especially important when you're fishing in shallow water, or working an area that gets a lot of fishing pressure. I feel that, with fishing pressure, fish eventually learn to identify the sound of an electric motor. Keeping the power on low reduces the chances of tipping off a trophy catch.

Another reason for running the electric on low power is a matter of common sense—boats don't have brakes. Every year I see anglers glide up to a fishing spot using their electric, being nice and quiet so the fish don't know they're there. And what happens is always the same—they glide up to the spot, they have time to fire off one cast, then they have to frantically crank on the motor and throw it into reverse, because their boat has continued gliding up to, and often right over, the spot they were fishing. Their quiet, stealthy approach is ruined because the boat kept gliding forward long after they shut off the motor. The powerful thrust of today's electrics can really blow out an area, almost like an underwater tornado. I've seen people ruin great spots like weed edges, or even crash into things like rocks, docks, and submerged stumps this way.

Remember that when you take your foot off the pedal or release the switch, you may turn off the electric motor, but the boat will continue to coast along, sometimes for a surprising distance. That's exactly why I run my motor on low power. As I'm approaching the target, it might take me a little bit longer to get to a spot, but I know I won't have to worry about coasting into it and spooking the fish. There's no question that the electric motor is one of the most important pieces of equipment in my boat!

CHAPTER 4

Tackle Tips

Belly Boats

Tip 56

Much of my fishing is from boats. There's no question I'm spoiled when it comes to having the cream of the crop. I use Lund aluminum and Ranger fiberglass fishing boats. Whether I'm fishing a tournament, big water trolling, or back trolling for bass and walleye, I've got it covered. And, I have a couple of small boats for going into remote back lakes, too. Of course, I'm lucky because a lot of anglers just don't have the room to keep a boat. The driveway is too small, there are already two or more cars, or they live in apartments and just don't have anywhere to park one. However, that doesn't mean they're landlocked. That's exactly where belly boats come in.

Belly boats are basically a truck inner tube wrapped in a tough, Cordura casing with a seat and some pockets for tackle. You pull on a pair of waders and sit in a belly boat just as you would sit in a lawn chair. Because you're in water from the waist down, you propel yourself with swim fins. The whole thing collapses down small enough to fit in the trunk of a small car, yet with one of those little air pumps you can find at Canadian Tire, you can inflate it from your vehicle's 12-volt power supply in just a few minutes.

Belly boats are not the choice for running and gunning, or traveling long distances. They're more for going into small areas and thoroughly fishing them, picking the cover apart to catch fish. You can get into tight situations, small bodies of water, or areas that aren't normally accessible by boat.

It seems that belly boats have taken off more in western Canada than in the east, but there are die-hards everywhere. I've fished with belly boats for walleye in Saskatchewan, and I know anglers in Ontario who fish backwoods ponds and even parts of the Great Lakes with them.

On a recent trip to British Columbia, we flew into a gorgeous lodge on Euksuk Lake, where the specialty is trout fishing from belly boats. There is great fishing on the main lake, but the lodge also offered fly-outs to other lakes nearby, one of which was known for exceptional rainbow trout fishing. We went at the first opportunity.

Picture this—we all have our fly rods and we're in our belly boats, surrounded by beautiful mountain peaks. Birds are singing; it's a gorgeous day. After about an hour or two of great fishing, I look out and see one of the guys out in the middle of the lake, in about a three inch chop on the water, just floating across the lake, not even casting. I was concerned and asked another person in our party if they thought he was all right out there. Turned out he was sound asleep—the sunshine, the quiet, the peaceful surroundings, and the gentle rocking of the belly boat sent him off to dreamland.

No one had fished this particular lake for about a year, and the fishing was absolutely superb. I caught my biggest trout of the afternoon just as the floatplane arrived to pick us up. As its pontoons touched the lake surface, a gorgeous rainbow came up and ate my dry fly off the surface, then went airborne the way rainbows do. I only managed to land the fish as the plane drew near. By then, I was ready for a nap myself. Tranquility at its finest!

Bladebaits

Tip 57

Bladebaits are uniquely versatile lures, in that they're effective both as search lures for locating fish in open water, and as finesse baits for surgically picking apart precise spots. Although they may not look like much—a flat piece of metal with a bean-shaped, lead body—bladebaits are extremely effective lures.

When it comes to covering water and trying to locate scattered fish, few lures can equal a blade. They cast like rockets and sink like stones, but they hold their depth once you start cranking the reel. So you can cover a lot of water with a bladebait, starting at the top and letting each successive cast sink a little deeper before you retrieve. It seldom takes long to find out how deep the fish are this way, and by allowing the same amount of time for the lure to sink on subsequent casts, you can put your lure right in front of them every time.

Consistent retrieves work most of the time, but you might want to experiment to see how fast or slow the fish want it on a given day. When they're active, or when you're fishing for competitive or schooling fish, fast retrieves generally work best. Similarly, slow retrieves are better when fish are less active or downright spooky.

Stop-and-go retrieves work well any time, especially for fish that tend to follow lures, like pike or coho. The little lure appears to stop suddenly and dive for bottom, then it zips away in a burst of speed, just like some small critter that knows it's being followed and is making a break for it. Hold on to your rod tightly, because the strikes that come are nothing short of explosive.

While casting is the easiest way to fish bladebaits, perhaps the best way is to jig them vertically. When you know exactly where the fish are, but need extra enticement to generate hits, then it's time to move to the B team.

Jigging bladebaits works best on deep, tightly schooled fish, or on fish moving along a known travel route. Simply drop the lure to the bottom (or to suspended fish you've marked on a fish finder) and pump it up and down. I usually start by sharply lifting the bait by about one foot, then I let it flutter back down on a slack line. However, it pays to experiment and see just what sort of action fish prefer from day to day—on occasion, fish will prefer presentations that are much more active or much more subtle. This technique can be deadly on lake trout.

Fish usually hit a bladebait as it sinks, so try to keep a reasonably tight line by lowering your rod tip as the lure sinks. Be careful not to keep too tight a hold, or you'll mess up the action. The trick is to watch your line for any sideways movement or abrupt bumps. If in doubt, set the hook anyway (I've always said hook sets are free, so why not?). Keep in mind that this is an all-metal lure, and most fish do not hold onto it for any length of time, so it's important to set the hook as quickly as you can. Using fluorescent-tinted lines can help detect light strikes. Some days you'll see more hits than you actually feel.

Jigging bladebaits isn't just an open water game—it's every bit as deadly through the ice. In fact, it's probably safe to say that in some areas, bladebaits are sold mainly as ice-fishing lures.

Regardless of whether you fish bladebaits through the ice or on open water, never tie them directly to your line, since the sharp metal body can slice monofilament like a knife. Instead, either add a split ring or, better yet, use a tiny, black, fine wire snap. They save your line from nicks and cuts and actually increase the lure's action by allowing more freedom of movement, especially when fishing with heavier lines.

Some bladebaits come with multiple eye holes that let you pick the action you prefer. Switching from one hole to another either tightens or opens up the wriggling action. Some days the fish get picky, and a bladebait will save you from a skunking.

Of course, the best way to learn each lure's ins and outs is to experiment. And considering how bladebaits catch fish, don't be surprised if you spend more time with them than you planned. They're not new, but they're still among the most versatile and effective lures on the market.

Buzzbaits

People often forget about buzzbaits when they think about topwaters because these baits don't float at rest like a standard topwater plug. But buzzbaits are among the best topwater lures available, especially when you have to cover a substantial amount of water and search for scattered fish.

Because they churn along with their single hook facing straight up, buzzbaits are among the most weedless of all topwaters—it takes pretty thick vegetation to clog them up. They're a great choice for fishing over huge weed flats that seem to go on and on forever, without any obvious spots for fish to hide. A friend of mine says they are the best fish finder he's ever owned, and for shallow situations, I have to agree they're tough to beat. Even if you don't actually hook the fish, you find out where it is and can follow up with another cast, or throw in a plastic worm or a jig instead.

But buzzbaits aren't merely shallow water baits. They're also effective for fishing deeper open areas for suspended smallmouth, or for pike and muskie heading out to their summer haunts on mid-lake shoals. Toss buzzbaits over any reefs or shoals connecting shallow spawning bays with the main lake basin, and you might be surprised how many big fish you catch out in the open.

Bob prefers buzzbaits that have been well broken in. Hold one out the truck window as you drive to accelerate the process. Once it starts to squeak, go fishing!

Buzzbaits come in a variety of styles, including two-blade, three-blade, or even twin-blade versions. In areas where the weeds aren't too heavy you can add a stinger hook to your buzzbait to help increase your hooking percentage. A single hook, with the point facing up, works in grassy bays and spots with scattered weeds. If I'm fishing in open water though, and where legal, I'll use an Excalibur treble hook instead. That usually solves short strike concerns right away!

I prefer longer soft action rods for buzzbait fishing because they help with hook sets at long distances. Holding the rod high during your retrieve not only helps keep the bait up at slow speeds, but also prevents you from setting the hook too fast. As with all topwater baits, the temptation with a buzzbait is to let the fish have it as soon as you see the hit. But it's better to wait a second to ensure that the fish actually has the bait in its mouth. With the rod up high, it takes you a bit of time to reel up slack line before setting the hook, and that extra time will increase your hooking percentage substantially.

Crankbaits

Take a walk down the aisle of any well-stocked tackle store and just for fun, start counting how many different shapes, sizes, and types of crankbaits you see. Chances are you'll be well into the dozens. Try the same thing in a couple of different stores and you could easily be into the hundreds.

Crankbaits—which dive as you crank the reel—are great lures and they catch tons of fish. But confronted with this vast, overwhelming selection, picking the ones that will work for you, on the lakes you fish, can be tough. Choosing the proper crankbaits is common sense.

Crankbaits catch fish for several reasons. One of the best things about them is that they work horizontally, so you can use them to cover quite a bit of water in a short time. The old saying about 90 percent of the fish living in just 10 percent of the water really is true, so the quicker you can find that magic 10 percent, the faster you'll start to catch something.

There are many other benefits to crankbaits. You can fish them at different speeds, from slow to fast, and you can fish them at a variety of

What makes a crankbait isn't its size, but the size of its lip. Here, side and top views show the lips of shallow- and deep-running Bomber crankbaits. The bigger the lip, the deeper the crankbait dives.

depths, from right on top of the water to way down deep. Crankbaits closely mimic the number one natural food of most predatory fish—minnows, perch, and other smaller fish. You can also find crankbaits that closely resemble crayfish or frogs. Some of these baits look so life-like they're positively scary.

Picking the right crankbait is a matter of considering the basics, which include depth, speed, action, material, buoyancy, and more. If you understand these factors, you're on easy street.

Let's look at depth first. Crankbaits are named as such because they dive when you crank the reel. Exactly how deep they go depends on several factors, but a quick guide is to look at the lip. As a rule, crankbaits with big lips dive deeper than those with little lips.

Some manufacturers, such as Bomber, sell what have become known as "series" crankbaits—the exact same lure offered in a number of different models, each with a progressively larger lip. You can buy the same lure in versions that run shallow, mid-depth, and deep.

Shallower-running lures such as the Cordell Big O feature squared-off lips, which are designed to allow you to bump the lure into rocks and logs without getting snagged. Crashing the lure into cover this way can be a deadly technique, especially when the fish develop lockjaw and ignore all else. The lip shape sends the lure bouncing away, rather than digging in.

Now let's look at speed. The lip style and size, along with the lure's body profile, will affect how quickly or slowly you can fish a given crankbait. Big lures with big lips can be worked fast, providing you're willing to crank like crazy and burn a lot of calories. Try working a big Hellbender at top speed for more than a few minutes. You'll be begging for a

But do crankbaits work? Just ask Bob's walleye— you can barely see the bait poking out of its mouth. Talk about down the hatch!

break. Yet fishing crankbaits fast can be a great way to catch fish. The trick, from the angler's perspective, is to select a lure you can work fast without wearing yourself out.

When it comes to action, crankbaits inevitably fall into one of two categories—wobblers and flashers. Wobbling crankbaits, such as the Bomber Long A, Rebel Crawfish, Cordell Big O, and Excalibur Fat Free Shad, display a violent left-right action when retrieved. Water moving over the lip forces the front of the bait from side to side, pointing the nose left, right, left, right as it jerks along. This throbbing action throws off enormous amounts of vibration and sound, making wobbling crankbaits ideal choices for use in low light periods or at night, in off-colored water, in and around weeds, or in any other situation where fish might not be able to see the lure right away. Models with integral rattles add even more noise and vibration.

Flasher-style crankbaits, such as the Cordell CC Shad, tend to throw off more flash and glare than a wobbler, while emitting less sound and thump. These lures rely more on visibility than vibration, moving along in a straighter, more direct path, with the body rolling to show more belly, less belly, more belly, less belly. They definitely have a tighter action. Flashers are often better than wobblers in high-visibility situations, such as when fishing a clear lake at midday, or when fishing for species such as pike that are primarily sight feeders. Flashers in toned-down, subtle colors can be just the trick for spooky fish that may shun the aggressive action of a wobbler. Sometimes the subtle approach works best.

Another consideration is buoyancy. Highly buoyant, floating crankbaits are great for those styles of fishing that follow a stop-and-go pattern. When you stop reeling, they pop back up to the surface. This can be a deadly technique when fishing over submerged weedbeds for largemouth bass, for example.

On the other end of the scale are zero-buoyancy models, which suspend at rest. They're better bets when fish are in a neutral or negative feeding mode, or when there's a lot of fishing pressure, or anytime fish are not in the mood to chase lures back to the surface.

There's one final consideration when picking crankbaits, which I haven't discussed yet, and that's profile. Generally, you want to use lures that will imitate the natural forage in a given lake or river. If the fish you're trying to catch feed on slender bait fish such as shiners, it makes sense to go with a slender crankbait, such as a Cordell Wally Diver. Where heavier-bodied prey are found, such as perch, use a heavier-bodied crankbait, such as a CC Shad or a Bomber Model A.

Getting Organized

Tip 60

If you're like most anglers, you feel you can never have enough fishing equipment. I thought I'd finally gotten to that point, then I went shopping and picked up some more things. You'd think a guy who's been in the business for more than 20 years would have enough tackle, but let's face it, a lot of companies out there are always building a slightly better mousetrap.

Buying tackle is one thing, but keeping track of it all is another. Sooner or later, organization becomes an issue for all anglers. In my line of work, which includes tournament fishing, shooting the TV series, and fishing for just about everything that swims all over the world, organizing tackle is not the easiest part of my job. What I've tried to do over the years (stress the word *tried*) is to keep ahead of the game by keeping everything modular. If I'm going to a bass tournament and I'm going to be fishing smallmouth bass 70 percent of the time and largemouth 30 per cent of the time, that's how I organize my tackle selection. If I'm going on a fly-in trip to a lake that has walleye, pike, lake trout, and a few grayling, it becomes more complex—especially when you have to keep within a certain weight allowance. How do you keep your tackle to a minimum and, at the same time, make sure you've got the essentials covered?

In many cases replacement tackle is not readily available, should you forget something important. On a fly-in, you can't just walk around the corner and drop into your local hardware store. The ideal situation is to be prepared and play it safe. What I mean by playing it safe is to have the basics. Let's take my hypothetical fly-in trip for walleye, pike, lake trout, and grayling as an example. On this trip, you'll have to take quite a few jigs, because in most northern situations there are areas with good old Canadian rock. An assortment of jigs would be my first priority because they'll catch just about everything that swims. And they're cheap—a big consideration when fishing places like rocky lakes, where you will probably lose a lot of lures. So you'll want to have a number of leadhead jigs, including a couple dozen eighth-ounce jigs (remember you're fishing for walleyes and grayling in shallow water), at least three dozen or more quarter-ounce jigs, and at least a couple dozen three-eighths-ounce jigs; that way you're covered regardless of the depth.

Got all the tackle, now where the heck do you put those donuts?

You'll also need lures that are going to go from top to bottom. For pike, take topwater baits, such as Zara Spooks or big buzzbaits, for exciting fishing. You might take 8 or 12 topwater baits in total.

You'll also want to bring a selection of crankbaits to cover depths from shallow to deep. Pack some versatile suspending baits, such as the Smithwick Rogue, as well. I would also bring a selection of spinnerbaits in case you wind up fishing for pike in the weeds. Keep in mind you're going to lose some lures on these trips, so you'll need spares of some of your real confidence lures. Because there are always people fishing with me on my trips (guests or camera crew), I carry more spares of every bait than I need so that we don't fall short when the fish are biting.

Finally, I'd bring some terminal tackle—hooks, weights, snaps, etc. You never know.

I carry tackle in a number of the small, hard plastic Plano boxes. There are a number of excellent hard plastic tackle boxes, as well as soft plastic ones such as the Tackle Logic system, so you can customize your selection for every trip. You take what you need by grabbing the correct boxes.

While working on this book, I took another look at my own tackle. Many anglers might be surprised to see what my tackle room looks like. Yes, I said room—not shelf or cupboard. It's probably the size of most medium-sized tackle stores. And, I'm sorry to say, it looks like it was hit by a hurricane. To get an idea, take three aisles of tackle from three different hardware stores, throw all the tackle in a room, and then hit the blender switch. That's what my room looks like. Other than that I consider myself quite an organized individual—just ask me!

Line Strength and Character

Tip 61

More misconceptions surround fishing line than any other item of fishing tackle. Perhaps the biggest confusion arises over strength. Why would anyone buy six-pound test line? What if you hook a seven-pound fish? Don't laugh—I wish I had a dollar for every time I've heard that.

The breaking strength of fishing line, of course, refers to how many pounds of tensile force it will withstand before breaking. It has nothing to do with the weight of the fish, which is why people can land 20-pound rainbow trout on six-pound line, or even 200-pound sharks on the same six-pound test. If you ever want to see some amazing feats, check out the International Game Fish Association's angling record book. The IGFA, along with the Freshwater Fishing Hall of Fame, keeps track not only of the biggest fish landed of each species, but also the heaviest landed on various line strengths. Some of the catches are absolutely unbelievable.

If your reel's drag is set correctly and your rod is held at the right angle to absorb the shock, it's difficult for most fish to break your line. Most break-offs happen when a fish jumps and lands on the line, perhaps snipping it with the sharp edge of a gill cover, or when a toothy critter such as a pike nicks your line or cuts it clean through. A line, previously abraded on a stick or rock, will also break easily. Other times, people may crimp a weight on too tightly or tie a bad knot. Fish are just one reason lines break.

I generally use Excalibur Silver Thread fishing line most of the time. It's a cofilament line, which means it utilizes two different compounds in its construction to provide reasonably low stretch limpness for easy casting and incredible abrasion resistance.

Determining which line strength is best for you is a matter of deciding which fish you want to catch, and what kind of conditions you will be fishing in. I've heard people snicker when I mention using 20- or 25-pound test line to catch bass, which, in all honesty, are normally two to three pounds in weight. They say it's overkill. But it really isn't when you look at the places I'm fishing. I only use this strength of line when I'm trying to hook bass in heavy cover, such as brush piles, intense weeds, or sunken duck blinds—the kind of places where you don't fight the fish, you just hook it and haul it out.

Most of the time I prefer to use the lightest line I can get away with. Lighter lines have smaller diameters than heavier lines, so they cast farther, sink faster, and allow lures to work deeper. They are also less visible to the fish than heavier lines. In open water conditions, I bet I would catch more fish on 8-pound test line than you would on 12-pound test line. This is especially true in clear water. As a case in point, for the past 30 years Great Lakes salmon fishermen have traditionally used 20- or 30-pound line when trolling for adult chinook salmon, which average about 22 to 25 pounds, and often pull the scales down well over the 30-pound mark. Yet in recent years, thanks to the increased clarity resulting from the zebra mussel invasion, the most successful anglers have been the ones running thin, clear 10-pound monofilament, which is far more difficult to detect than that thicker, heavy stuff. Thinner line means more hits.

Light lines are also a plus when you're dealing with spooky fish. This is why so many Great Lakes steelhead fishermen have adopted long, light action rods and four-pound monofilament as a standard. The super-thin mono is difficult for the fish to see, so their presentations look far more convincing. The long, light rods give them the leverage to fight the fish, while absorbing the energy that would otherwise break such light line in a fight.

Most fishermen have a story about the big one that broke their line and got away, but I know a guy who has a better tale—the big one that broke off and still got caught. The guy is my good friend Tom Brooke, who is the general manager of Shimano Canada. Tom was fishing on Lake Erie, during his first Canadian Open bass tournament. My brother Wayne was fishing beside him on a shoal, when Wayne looked over and saw Tom fighting a big smallmouth that had gone down behind the boat. Then it seemed Tom had broken off the fish.

A few seconds later this fish jumps at the back of Tom's boat. Apparently the line had caught in between the motor mount and the hull of the boat. The line broke but remained stuck to the boat, with the bass still solidly hooked. Tom realized what had happened, reached down and grabbed the line, then hand-bombed the fish into the boat. It turned out to be their biggest fish of the day. Ironic that a guy who works for the Shimano fishing rod company winds up catching fish by hand.

Lipless Crankbaits

Tip 62

There's no question that lipless crankbaits are one of my favorite types of lures—they are easy to use, and they consistently catch fish. You simply cast them out and reel them back in. Well, actually, there's more than this to lipless crankbaits, or rattlebaits as some anglers call them. These lures vibrate rapidly on the retrieve and create quite a bit of noise with their internal rattles. These characteristics make them excellent search lures if you're fishing over a broad area.

When fish are actively feeding, "burning" these lures, a term used to describe retrieving them as fast as you can turn the reel handles, is often the best approach. Other times, a stop-and-go retrieve works better. You have to experiment and see what's most effective on a given day.

Lipless crankbaits are, for the most part, open water lures. Most sink on a slack line, at a rate of about a foot per second, which makes it easy to count them down to the depth you want to fish. For instance, if the fish are 15 feet down, you cast out, count to 15, and then start reeling. Simplicity plus.

Other lipless crankbaits are made to be neutrally buoyant, so they suspend at rest. These are particularly effective on a stop-and-go

The Cordell Spot is one of Bob's all-time favorite lures.

retrieve, as they just hang there in the water when you stop. Often times fish will sit there, mesmerized, and pounce on the lure as soon as it moves again. A stop-and-go retrieve also works very well when fishing lipless crankbaits through weeds.

I've caught many large northern pike in the midsummer this way. I often search for fresh green cabbage weed and burn a Cordell Spot right through it. When I feel the Spot has quit vibrating and fouled in weeds, I'll rip it free with a sharp snap of the wrist, which often triggers a strike.

Years ago I was fishing the St. Lawrence River in Montreal, working a shipping channel that had a good weedline bordering the deeper water. I was fishing in a bass tournament and had located some smallmouth that were mixed with some big pike. Bass bold enough to mix with pike are generally larger bass, so I was optimistic. For every bass I caught I'd catch at least 10 to 15 pike. I can remember catching 2 good bass after weeding through 20 to 30 large northerns that were all 10 to 15 pounds apiece. It was a lot of fun.

Of course lipless crankbaits aren't just for smallmouth and pike. I've caught virtually everything on them—brook trout, lake trout, rainbow trout, salmon, muskie, largemouth, walleye, striped bass, Arctic grayling, and several saltwater species too.

I'll never forget a particular fishing expedition with my brother Wayne down in Florida. He caught two decent-sized largemouths, both at the same time, on a Cordell Rattle Spot. Spots typically drive fish to hit them hard—they try to kill them, rather than just inhale them smoothly. This time, two bass tried their best and both got hooked on the Spot's twin treble hooks. I've since caught two fish on a single cast with lipless crankbaits at home in Canada. Because of the competitive nature of predator fish, these rattling, vibrating, fast-moving baits will always be a staple in my tackle box.

Lure Colors

The selection of lure colors can be overwhelming. When a new type of lure comes out it's often offered in dozens of different colors. This can be confusing. Which one should you buy? Confidence plays a role, no doubt. If I find that a particular color combination is working well, I can become stubborn about it just like anyone else. If a color has worked well for you in the past, you'll probably have more confidence in it and, as a result, fish harder with it. It can be worthwhile trying funky new lure colors, if only because the fish haven't seen them yet. They could increase your strike percentage.

Color can certainly represent the difference between numerous bites and no bites at all. I've seen this demonstrated countless times, but never so vividly as when salmon fishing on the Great Lakes. When offshore trolling for chinook and coho, it's common practice to run several lines with identical lures in different colors. Often, all the fish will be caught on one rod using one color of lure. This hap-

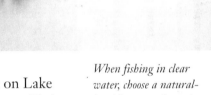

When fishing in clear water, choose a natural-hued lure, one that mimics real prey.

pened recently while I was trolling for late-season chinook on Lake Ontario with Prairie Oyster fiddle player John P. Allen, his son Taylor, and my son Darren. We trolled for about two or three hours, and caught five chinooks and a beautiful steelhead just under 20 pounds, all on one chartreuse and white spoon. We trolled an identical blue and white spoon right beside it—at the same speed—and never got a hit. That particular day, it had to be green.

If you've been fishing for quite a while you might remember a product sold in the '80s called a Lake Systems Color-C-Lector. It was a gadget with a probe on the end of a wire cable. When lowered into the water, it would suggest the most visible lure color. Once when my brother Wayne and I were fishing in one of the early Pro Bass tournaments, I

When fishing in off-color or muddy water, choose a gaudy-hued lure, one that will be easy for the fish to locate.

hauled the Color-C-Lector out and it told us to use a red lure. I had a flipping jig with black and red rubber tied on to it. I put it on with some pork rind and proceeded to catch two bass on back-to-back casts—one was five pounds, the other just under—and, as a result, went on to win the tournament. Was it the color that instigated the strike? I can't say, but I did catch two very large bass on a color I normally wouldn't use.

Generally, I select lure color according to what the fish are feeding on. It isn't always the right choice, but it's a good starting point. Suppose, for example, we're fishing a river for trout. If it has a rocky bottom, the fish could be gorging themselves on tiny crayfish or insect larvae like mayflies, caddis flies, or stone flies. In this situation, I'd start fishing a fairly small lure with subtle browns, blacks, and greens. On the other hand, in many of the big, open water circumstances, I'll generally go with natural, fishlike colors to try and imitate baitfish.

The only time I tend to avoid this approach is when fishing in stained or off-color water. In such water, fish can't see very far and they have trouble picking out dull, natural-finish lures. This is when I choose bright or fluorescent lures that penetrate the dingy water and give the fish a more defined target to zero in on.

Minnowbaits

Tip 64

Minnowbaits are one of the more versatile lures available. Closely resembling real baitfish, they can be twitched, jerked, trolled, or just reeled in with a steady retrieve. They come with big lips, little lips, and shallow to deep running lips. Some sink, some float, while still others suspend. In size, they range from two inches to more than a foot in length. It's this variety that makes them such great lures. This, and the fact that the number one food item for most species of fish is smaller fish.

Things to consider regarding minnowbaits are their overall lure size, the depth they can attain, and the type of action they have in the water. The overall lure size is a no-brainer—just look at the bait itself. If anglers make one mistake though, it's that many times we use lures that are too small. This is especially true when angling for large, predatory fish such as pike. A 10-pound pike is a nice fish, not a giant, but a decent-sized fish. Most people would look at a 10-pound pike and suggest that a lure in the four- to six-inch range is appropriate. Yet if you talk with biologists, they'll tell you a pike is capable of eating prey up to 20 percent of its own size. This means a 10-pound pike can eat a 2-pound walleye. The 2-pound wall-eye, in turn, is bigger than a four- to six-inch minnowbait.

Minnowbaits are one of the most popular lure varieties for two simple reasons. One, they come in a huge variety of styles, and two, they work!

When selecting minnowbaits for size, I also like to pay attention to what the normal forage is. If perch are the principal baitfish, then it makes sense to use a lure that closely mimics perch in size and profile. If you are fishing for pike in shallow water, or if it's early spring and they're gorging themselves on three-inch minnows, then these are also things to consider. Post-spawn pike readily eat smaller lures since these fish are still in the recovery process.

The depth and action a given minnowbait will develop can be told in part by the location, shape, and size of the diving lip. Big lips displace more water than smaller lips, so they make the lure go deeper. Lures with very big lips, such as the Rebel Spoonbill Minnow, dive far deeper than a regular Rebel Minnow, which is basically the same lure with a smaller lip.

Certain minnowbaits have unique actions that give them an edge in specific conditions. For example, the Bomber Long A series has a wobbling action; they move from side to side, with a lot of vibration. This series may include built-in rattles for extra attraction, making them great baits when fish are actively chasing prey, or for fishing in low-light conditions, where fish may have a tough time finding them by vision alone.

Other minnowbaits, such as the Smithwick Rogue, tend to roll more than wobble. They generate a lot of flash in the water, closely imitating an injured baitfish—so much so that many such baits are now sold in suspending versions for an even more lifelike presentation. They're great for fish such as pike and salmon, which hunt primarily by sight. You can fish these lures a bit faster than a wobbling type, which makes them awesome for covering a lot of water in a short time. Both varieties—the rolling and the wobbling—are available in jointed versions, which offer an even more exaggerated action. They're tough to beat when fish are picky and need that little extra to convince them to hit.

It doesn't matter whether I'm fishing a major tournament or heading away on a remote fly-in, I always make sure I have a good selection of different minnowbaits. They work for virtually all species and are too versatile to leave behind.

Poppers

Tip 65

Of the artificial lures, poppers are one of the newest, hottest types and, at the same time, one of the oldest types. Surface poppers, such as the Rebel Pop-R and the Arbogast Hula Popper, have been around for decades, yet they still catch fish—especially bass.

Poppers are the slowpokes of the topwater baits. You retrieve them in a steady stop-and-go (or pop-and-stop) motion. Depending on the mood of the fish, you might pause anywhere from 5 to 30 seconds between pops. Actually, pop is the perfect word to describe the action—you just give a quick flick of your rod tip and "pop" the lure forward about six inches or so. Needless to say, it can take quite a while to complete a retrieve on a long cast.

If you know the fish are on the spot but suspect they're just being uncooperative, you can try a tournament tactic called deadsticking. To do this, you just cast the popper onto the spot, pop it once, and do nothing else. You let it sit dead still (hence the name) and you play a waiting game. This is when that old saying about curiosity killing the cat comes into play. Eventually, even the toughest fish will crack and plaster the bait.

When fishing poppers in shallow water, long casts are a big advantage. While many poppers are heavy enough to cast on a baitcasting outfit, a long, soft action rod will provide hook setting and fish-fighting power at long distances. Longer rods will aid casting distance in the wind while picking up more line on the hook set.

Bob Izumi lands a dandy smallmouth bass on his favorite popper—a Rebel Pop-R.

Tip 66 • Propeller Baits

Propeller baits, such as the Heddon Dying Flutter or Tiny Torpedo, are two of the oldest topwater lures available. Each bait looks like a little cigar with a propeller at one or both ends. As you pull the baits forward, the propeller turns, creating a huge amount of noise. These are incredible baits for calling smallmouth up from deep water, or for use when there's a little bit of a chop on the water.

My brother Wayne has been a Tiny Torpedo fan for years, and has caught some truly enormous bass on these baits. They're appealing because they're small and make an enormous commotion in the water. Big bass eat these baits as if they were live and not artificial.

Propeller baits can be worked with either a straight continuous retrieve, fast or slow, or in a slow stop-and-go fashion. Bass seem to prefer stop-and-go, with pauses of 10 to 15 seconds between short pulls. Muskie, on the other hand, seem to prefer a continuous fast retrieve.

Propeller baits are ideal, audible lures for night fishing, especially on dark, overcast evenings.

Rods and reels for propeller baits should have a light tip action, since they're small lures and you'll want to throw them quite a distance.

Retrieving Spoons

Cast them out and reel them back in. This is the way 99 percent of fishermen retrieve spoons. And really, it's too bad, because there are dozens of great ways of doing this.

One of my favorite ways of retrieving spoons is to cast a single hook, weedless spoon with a pork frog trailer and let it settle to the bottom. Then, I pop it off and let it flutter back down, so it imitates a crayfish. It's deadly on bass and pike.

Another variation is to look for cover, such as stumps, boulders, and dock pilings, cast a spoon well past the object, then retrieve it so it comes as close as possible to the object. When it's just about scraping the object, stop reeling and let the spoon flutter down. This is often the key to triggering thunderous strikes.

Speaking of explosive action, this is what you get when you buzz a spoon across the surface of thickly matted weeds.

And if you really want to see the water go flying, toss a weedless spoon into a bed of lily pads and try to skitter it up onto one of the big leaves. Just let it lie there for a minute or two before you ease it off the pad back into the water.

Let's not forget that one of the best spoon retrieves is no retrieve at all. It consists of jigging the lure up and down off the side of your boat or through a hole in the ice. Just pop the spoon up a foot or so with your rod tip and let it flutter back down on a moderately slack line.

Rigging up with a snap, to add a little extra noise to your lure on the retrieve, can also pay dividends. I'll never forget fishing with Wayne in a bass tournament a few years ago. On this occasion, we were fishing muddy water in big, thick, isolated lily pad patches for largemouth bass. Wayne chose to fish with a silver Heddon Moss Boss, a plastic spoon that rides upright on the retrieve. Wayne's Moss Boss was old and well worn, to the point that the little snap on the lure's front end would actually make a squeaking sound as he twitched it back to the boat. But, by twitching it along in a fast, stuttering motion with his rod tip, he could get a skittering action on the surface of the lily pads and the spoon would squeak every time he twitched it. He caught a couple of very large bass before I switched to a Moss Boss, and we walked away with that tournament. The

Moss Boss memories! Bob comes to grips with a 20-pound-plus northern pike from northern Saskatchewan's Cree River, caught by swimming a Moss Boss through thick cover.

squeaking noise of the spoon was calling those fish up from under the lily pads in the murky water.

So, just cast them out and reel them back? No way, folks. Spoons are some of the most versatile lures in your tackle box. Just remember to let your imagination run wild when it comes to retrieves.

Rod Action

Many fishermen, especially those just starting out, find it difficult to understand what is meant by the term "rod action." So, let's make everybody a pro on the subject. Rod action refers to the way in which a rod will bend under pressure. You can roughly categorize rods into one of three styles—light, medium, or heavy action.

The easiest way to understand these different styles, and to size up the action of a rod when you're in a tackle shop, is to carry a 10- or 15-foot piece of monofilament fishing line in your pocket. Snug one end of the line against the rod handle and string the other end up through the guides. Then, ask someone to hold onto the dangling piece.

Bob's light-action steel-head rod bends evenly from butt to tip. Rod designers call this a parabolic action, and it's great for fishing with light line.

When you pull back on a heavy-action rod, you will notice that it hardly bends or flexes at all. Now, do the same thing with a light-action rod. Observe how the whole rod bends. A medium-action rod, on the other hand, lies halfway between these two extremes in terms of flexibility.

String your line through a medium-action rod and you'll notice that most of the flexibility is confined to the upper third of the rod, while the middle third barely bends, and the bottom third is rigid and firm.

In the past couple of years, rod manufacturers have made incredible advances in fishing rod performance. More complex tapers, new materials, and new assembly methods have allowed rod builders to build rods that seem to defy categorization. So rather than lumping their sticks into the light, medium, and heavy categories, some manufacturers and anglers now look at rods with specific fishing techniques in mind. Rather than thinking, "Gee, this is a nice medium-action rod," people are now thinking, "Gee, this is a great spinnerbait rod."

I have to admit that as a tackle junkie I like to experiment with different rod actions for specific fishing techniques. Because I've been in this business for more than two decades, the folks at Shimano have asked me to design a series of rods. So far I have come up with almost 20 different rod actions, most of them geared to specific techniques and situations, rather than to the old categories of light, medium, and heavy. For example, when fishing topwater lures such as Pop-Rs, or light crankbaits with treble hooks, I prefer a soft tip rod that won't pull the lure away from the fish. With a spinnerbait rod, I like a bit of backbone, but also a bit of softness in the tip, so that the fish engulfs the spinnerbait before I feel it.

Longer fishing rods have become more common over the years. Some muskie anglers have now started using rods that are up to eight feet in length. For many years bass anglers have used rods as long as seven and a half feet in length for pitching or flipping. A longer rod gives you more leverage for hook sets and at the same time makes it easier to pick up any slack line. A longer rod also allows you to gain extra casting distance. In the clear water so typical of many North American lakes, this alone is a big advantage.

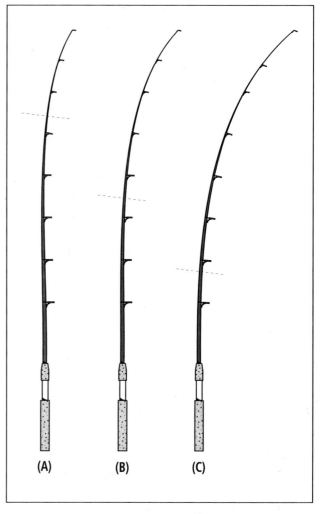

(A) (B) (C)

A fast-action rod (A) provides the best sensitivity and hook-setting power, while a light-action rod (C) provides the greatest ability to absorb shock and prevent break-offs when fishing with light lines. A medium-action rod (B) represents a compromise between these features.

Last but not least, the hooks that you use can dictate the rod action that you'll need. For example, small, thin diameter wire hooks will penetrate a fish's mouth with minimal force, allowing you to use a softer action rod. But if you're using a lure with thicker diameter hooks, you'll need a stiffer action rod to allow a harder hook set. This is why I often have so many rods in the boat—they all do different things. Just as a golfer uses a driver to cover long distances and a putter for more precise shots, or a carpenter uses large, coarse nails for construction and fine finishing nails for attaching trim, anglers select rods based on what they need them to do. If you're fishing with a lure with a heavy hook on it, like a flipping jig, it's obvious that you'll need a heavier action rod than when you're using a small crankbait with fine wire hooks.

Slip Floats

Tip 69

Slip floats do exactly as their name suggests. Unlike a conventional float or bobber, which attaches to the fishing line with a spring or a chunk of elastic tubing and is held fixed in one position, slip floats attach via a hollow tube or ring arrangement that allows them to slide freely up and down along the line.

Before attaching a slip float, you first attach a small item called a bobber stop to your line. The bobber stop, which is usually nothing more than a small bead, is large enough not to pass through the float, but small enough to travel through your fishing rod's line guides and spool onto the reel. The bobber stop allows you to set your float so that it holds your bait at various depths.

For instance, say you mark some large fish on your sonar suspended at 23 feet in 40 feet of water. Simply slide the bobber stop 23 feet up the line from your hook. Reel up the slack line, cast as normal, and watch as 23 feet of line slide through the float, dropping your hook down to the fish. At that magic 23-foot mark, the bobber stop meets the float and, being too large to pass through the hole, jams in place, cocking the bobber up vertically. This is as good as it gets when you need a precise depth presentation. Your bait is nose-to-nose with the fish. Cast after cast, you'll always be at that 23-foot level.

You just can't do this with a normal float. Try making a cast with 23 feet of line dangling below your bobber. You can't do it. This is the beauty of a slip float. You can cast normally, yet reach fish at any depth whatsoever.

While slip floats are normally used by anglers fishing with live baits, I find they're incredibly useful with certain types of artificial lures as well. Pretty much any type of lure or bait you can use in a vertical presentation will work beneath a slip float.

Take jigs for example. Because your line isn't fixed in a single position, you can use the float to help impart action to a twist-tail grub or a tube. Snap your rod back, and line will slide through the float, lifting the jig in the water. Drop your rod and feed back slack line, and the jig falls back down to the fish. This is a deadly technique when fishing with grubs or tubes, which wriggle or spiral on the drop.

I observed this firsthand while fishing at central Quebec's La Reserve Beauchene for smallmouth bass a couple of years ago, with legendary float fisherman Mick Thill. Rigged up with slip floats, we caught several nice bass by fishing behind other anglers, fishing the same spots they had already worked over—unsuccessfully—with standard baits and presentations. Where they failed to draw a hit, we caught fish. That was all it took to convince me of the value of slip floats. They can be a natural, subtle presentation.

Sometimes when you begin catching fish on slip floats, other anglers will try to copy you by rigging up with bobbers of their own. But unless they have a sharp eye, they won't realize your float is a *slip* bobber. One acquaintance of mine, who has been fishing slip bobbers for years, told me about a time he was hammering steelhead in the Niagara River, fishing the fast water at the Whirlpool Rapids. He hooked several fish on roe fished 15 feet beneath a slip bobber. Other anglers nearby also decided to rig up with bobbers. When they saw him cast, they noticed his bobber only two feet up the line from the bait, so that's where they set their fixed floats. What they didn't notice was that a dozen feet of line actually slid through his float before it cocked up in the water. While he continued to catch fish, they drifted 12 feet above the fish and could only scratch their heads in wonder. Not one person asked him what he was doing to hook the fish.

Spinning Tackle versus Baitcasting Gear

Tip 70

I've talked about this on my television show and in my seminars, but I continue to be asked which I prefer, spinning gear or baitcasting equipment. This is a difficult question to answer because there are times when spinning gear works best, and other times when a baitcasting outfit is a better choice. Which one I reach for depends on how I'm fishing.

As a general rule, baitcasting equipment works best when you need to use heavier lines and larger lures, or when you need to pull strong fish from heavy cover. Although there are baitcasting reels that will handle 8- and 10-pound line, for the most part the average angler would have an easier time casting lighter line with a spinning outfit. Baitcasting outfits work best when you're dealing with lines from 12- to 30-pound test. Baitcasting reels tend to handle heavy lines better than spinning reels, partly due to the way the spool is oriented to the rod. The line peels off a baitcasting reel's revolving spool evenly, whereas thick, heavy monofilament tends to coil as it comes off a spinning reel's fixed spool, making it tougher to cast. The only way to avoid this is to move up to a saltwater-sized spinning reel, which will handle heavier lines.

Baitcasting outfits allow you to easily feather the spool on the cast, which makes them ideal for those times, say, when flipping or pitching, when you need accuracy. It takes a bit of practice to learn how to do this, but once you master it, you can plop casts into precise areas without making any kind of splash at all—perfect for big fish in shallow cover.

The other big plus with baitcasting outfits is that you can buy wide-spool versions of most reels, for extra line capacity. That's just one reason they're so popular for trolling. Other baitcasting reels built especially for trolling situations even have little line counters built into them, so you know how much line you have out. This is a big help when dealing with spooky fish. If you find you get more hits when your lure is 120 feet back of the boat, you can consistently repeat the pattern by zeroing the counter and then letting out 120 feet of line.

Spinning outfits cover the opposite end of the spectrum—they work best when dealing with lighter lines and lighter weight lures, or when distance is your biggest concern. Because the spool on a spinning reel doesn't turn on the cast, it's unbeatable at casting super-light lures or for casting into the wind without fear of tangling. Spinning reels are easy to use and are the best choice for beginners.

Spinning outfits work best with lines of 10-pound test or less. Of course you can buy heavy-duty spinning rigs for muskie fishing or for saltwater use, which handle lines up to 40-pound test. But they can be cumbersome for most freshwater fishing situations. Most spinning rods and reels are designed to work best with monofilament line, ranging from four- to eight-pound test.

Heavier lines can be tough to cast on spinning gear, especially in cold weather. Monofilament lines develop memory with time (especially in the cold), so instead of flowing off the spool smoothly and evenly, the line springs off in big coils, which do not flow through the guides very well. In fact, this is the reason spinning rods have such large guides—to try and funnel those big line coils down the rod as smoothly as possible.

Baitcasting gear is the best choice for tough work, like fishing for pike and largemouth bass in heavy cover, for trolling, or when using heavy lures and lines.

Spinning outfits can be very accurate in the hands of a practiced caster. Long, powerful spinning rigs are the best choice when you need maximum distance, such as when surf fishing from shore, or when tossing spoons from a pier for salmon and lake trout. Fishing clear water offers another opportunity to use a longer rod.

One question I'm often asked about spinning reels is, "Which is better, front or rear drag?" Both systems work well—it's a matter of personal preference. Rear drag systems are much easier to adjust while fighting a fish. Some people like to be able to back off the drag or tighten it as conditions dictate. Shimano took this concept one step further several years ago when they introduced their Fightin' Drag system, which consists of a lever in addition to the drag knob, so that you can easily fine-tune the drag with a flick of your finger while fighting a fish. This reel has become very popular.

Front drag reels are not as convenient to adjust as rear drag reels, but they tend to be smoother, partly because the drag washers can be made a bit larger. Front drags are most popular with anglers who fish for species such as salmon and steelhead that make repeated long runs. Depending on whom you talk to, some anglers say a front drag is smoother. If you ever need to apply extra drag pressure in a fight with a big fish, you can gently use your fingertip to feather the edge of the line spool. But easy does it! Don't touch it too firmly or you risk breaking off the fish! This little trick works well, but it takes time to develop the correct feel for it.

Bob prefers spinning gear for fishing with light lures and lines of 10-pound test or less.

Stinger Hooks

Tip 71

You know the fish are nearby because they're boiling behind your lure. Or they're stripping the bait clean from your hook. But the problem is, they're striking short, and you're having trouble setting the hook. So what's a frustrated angler supposed to do? Add a stinger hook, and fast. This is a trick I often use when fishing noisy lures, such as buzzbaits and spinnerbaits, in muddy water or across the tops of weeds.

What often happens in hard-to-see situations such as these is that the fish sense your lure whirling past them. But when they lunge for it, they miss it completely. Or manage to grab only the tail. By adding a stinger hook, you can turn most of these short strikes into solid hookups. Stingers can make a major difference—you may catch half a dozen fish and five of these may be hooked on the trailer hook alone.

A stinger is really just a second hook that trails behind your lure. True stinger hooks, made for spinnerbaits and buzzbaits, are easy to spot. They're made with big, wide, open eyes, which slip easily over the point and barb of your main hook. I like the Lindy style, in which the eyes are coated in a rubbery compound to keep them from slipping off, or the Strike King variety, which are held in place with a piece of soft tubing. Without something to hold the stinger hook in place, you risk hooking the fish but losing the hook. Another option is to open the eye of the trailer hook with a pair of pliers and then pinch it back to normal around the main hook. This will hold it on for good.

For a number of years now I've been using the larger sizes of Excalibur treble hooks as stingers when fishing spinnerbaits for smallmouth, pike, and muskie in open water. I just stretch a chunk of surgical tubing over the hook eye, then hook it on my bait. The treble seems to up your percentages of fish, especially if they're nipping at the bait in the way smallmouth do. When fishing spinnerbaits and buzzbaits in cover, I'll stick to the single hook. Always, always, with the point facing up.

Adding a stinger hook to buzzbaits, spinnerbaits, and even jigs can turn short-strikers into solid hookups.

Walleye anglers have refined stingers over the years, and today there are several versions of the same basic rig—a very short leader of monofilament tied to a tiny treble hook. These are great when you tip jigs with minnows, since the soft monofilament doesn't detract from the minnow's effectiveness and still allows a hook point far back on the body.

Many trout and walleye fishermen have adapted a West Coast steelhead rig, in which two single hooks are tied in tandem, about four inches apart. While the BC steelheaders use it with gobs of spawn for ocean-running steelhead and salmon, eastern anglers find it's a deadly setup for worm fishing, especially when walleye, steelhead, or big brown trout are being fussy and only nipping at the bait.

When rigging stingers, especially those involving treble hooks, make sure you don't accidentally exceed the number of hooks you are permitted by law. Where I live in Ontario, the law allows four hooks in total, so my single-hook spinnerbait and treble-hook stinger are okay. But that's not the case everywhere, and regulations do change from time to time. Always make a point of checking first.

Sunglasses

Tip 72

During the summer I am constantly ribbed about my reverse suntan. When I'm on the water fishing, I always wear polarized sunglasses, so I end up having a tanned face, with light patches over my eyes, where the sunglasses block the sun. I kind of look like a reverse raccoon. I don't care, though, because I refuse to spend that much time on the water without my polarized sunglasses. They protect my eyes from damage due to excessive ultraviolet (UV) light exposure, they protect me from physical damage should a fish shake the lure at boatside, and they actually help me catch more fish.

Let's look at ultraviolet light exposure first. Scientists divide UV light into three broad categories based on wavelength—UVA, UVB and UVC. UVC light is generally filtered out by the atmosphere, so there's no problem with it. But this is not the case with the short-length UVB, and UVA rays. They're the ones that burn and/or tan your skin, and over time, they can do the same thing to the lining of your eyeballs. This doesn't sound like fun, does it?

How long does it take? That depends on the individual and where you are fishing. UV is strongest at high altitudes, weakest at sea level. Even the color of your eyes can make a difference. Light-colored eyes let in more UV than dark ones.

Even if you're not suffering UV bombardment, a day on a boat, squinting through strong light, will give anyone a headache. Why give yourself a headache when you can avoid it by wearing good quality sunglasses?

Besides, sunglasses offer you a level of protection from impact damage. You never know when accidents will happen. I've had fish shake the hook and force me to duck many times, just as I've slipped on the path along the creek now and then, and caught a faceful of branches for my trouble. Last year while competing in a team tournament with my brother, Wayne, I decided to swing a small bass, weighing about a pound, over the gunnels rather than netting it or reaching down to grab it. In midair, with the rod loaded like a slingshot, the ½-ounce jig pulled free and hit me square in the left lens of my glasses. To this day I keep the glasses as a reminder of how lucky I am to have both eyes. Your eyes won't grow back if you hurt them, so it makes sense to protect them any way you can.

It's not the main reason I wear them, but sunglasses can help you to spot fish. And, even if you don't see the fish themselves, sunglasses are great for spotting drop-offs and fish cover, such as weedlines, scattered boulders, or stumps.

Former Toronto Blue Jay Pat pitcher Hentgen uses polarized sunglasses to spot fish-holding cover and, as a result, catches plenty of chunky large-mouth bass.

When it comes to buying a pair of sunglasses for fishing, use different criteria than you would for shades worn playing golf or driving. Lenses come in two basic materials—glass and plastic. Glass gives the best optical quality and clarity, but it's also expensive and relatively heavy. Good plastic or polycarbonate lenses, on the other hand, are almost as optically correct as glass and they're more resistant to fogging. The only real downside to plastic lenses is that they're a bit easier to scratch.

Green or gray lenses are the most popular because these tints do not radically affect color perception. But I also like to carry a pair of sunglasses with amber lenses, for fishing in overcast weather, in the rain, or at dawn or dusk when the light is dim. Amber-tinted lenses make everything appear lighter and improve contrast.

Of course, good frames are just as important as good lenses, and you need to consider more than cosmetics and individual taste. Plastic frames are as light as wire but tend to be more comfortable in cold weather.

You can't put a price tag on your sight, so good fishing glasses are an important and worthwhile investment. Besides, anything that helps you to stay comfortable and to catch fish is worth it—even if it does make you look like a reverse raccoon. The bottom line is I don't leave home without my polarized fishing glasses.

Tube Bait Additives

Tip 73

Tube jigs are undoubtedly one of the most dependable artificial lures available. It seems that when fish refuse everything else, they can still be caught on tubes. Yet even tubes can be improved, and adding stuff to a tube bait can definitely increase its effectiveness.

Giving the bait a squirt of commercial scent attractant such as Pradco's Real Craw never hurts. Whether attractants catch more fish because they add an alluring scent, or simply because they cover up the human odor, remains undetermined. It's a moot point though—what matters is that they increase the number of bites you get.

Pouring the stuff directly over the surface of the tube works fine, but you can do even better by stuffing a tiny piece of sponge inside the bait first. Then, squirt the scent inside. The sponge helps to hold the scent.

Similarly, inserting a piece of Styrofoam causes the bait to float up in the water, making it sink far more slowly and, therefore, making it more effective for reluctant biters, such as cold-water walleye. You can add other materials as well. One old tournament technique that still works well today is to break off a piece of an Alka Seltzer tablet and place it inside the tube bait's hollow body. The lure will give off a trail of bubbles as you work it through the water.

I remember fishing in a bass tournament at Long Point on Lake Erie a couple of years ago with John Vandivier. We were fishing for largemouth on this shallow, sandy flat, in no more than two feet of water. I saw this black shadow, which turned out to be a very large fish, swimming some distance ahead of the boat. We motored over to it very quietly with the electric motor on low power to avoid spooking it. The fish was a largemouth bass—black as a piece of coal, with a huge head, fins, and tail, and a skinny body. Its eyes appeared to be glazed over as well, making it look a little like a walleye. If I hadn't known better I would have thought it was some kind of sea bass, it was so strange looking. I later learned that the fish was probably blind. Fish take on coloration to match their surroundings, so this bass should have been light colored, to match the sandy area it was swimming over. Instead, it couldn't see, so it was very dark in appearance.

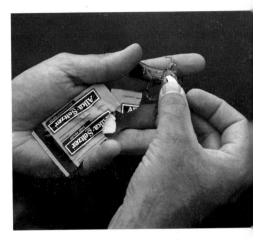

An old tournament trick, but still a winner— adding a chunk of an Alka Seltzer tablet to your tube jig makes it fizz in the water. The bubbles attract curious fish and can elicit bites you wouldn't otherwise get.

Anyway, we followed this bass for several minutes, casting all sorts of lures at it, trying to get it to hit. I rummaged around in the boat, found a little bit of Alka Seltzer, and stuffed it inside a tube jig. I then cast the tube a couple of feet in front of the bass.

Moving slowly, the bass wandered along, made its way to the jig, tilted up its head, and sucked it in. I set the hook, John got the net, and it turned out to be the biggest fish of the tournament at just under five pounds. Had the fish been blessed with normal vision, it probably would have weighed six or seven pounds. It had the head and skeletal features to suggest this.

The old Alka Seltzer trick still works wonders, but additives for tube baits have come a long way. The latest goodie to hit the market is a product called Crackle, which looks like one of those tablets you take when you have a cold. Crackle is said to make tubes sound like crayfish. Does it work? I can't say, but several tournaments have been won by anglers fishing tube jigs with Crackle. My belief is that tube jig additives are much like scents. Do they work? Only probably. But they certainly don't hurt your odds. Only the fish know for sure.

Tube Rigging for Special Occasions

Tip 74

Tube jigs are great lures for neutral or even turned-off fish. Unfortunately, these spooky fish often sit tightly in heavy cover, such as at the base of weedlines or in downed trees, where fishing a tube jig can be incredibly frustrating. As the lure spirals on its way down, it hangs up on everything.

A wide-gapped offset hook can be rigged for heavy cover. Similarly to Texas rigging with a plastic worm, you simply thread the hook through the head of the tube and bring it out about ⅓ of an inch. Then bring it back around, line up the tube, and poke the hook through both

When rigging tubes on weedless jig heads, thread the bait onto the hook guard first, then pop the hook eye through the bait in the regular manner.

walls of the tube. Gently stick the point in the wall of the tube to prevent it from snagging.

Another option is to use a weedless jig head. You rig a tube on a weedless hook by first feeding the hook guard up into the lure body, then poking it through near the front of the bait. Follow the hook guard with the hook itself, and poke the eye out the front of the tube. Tie your line on as normal, then slip the hook eye backward so that it rests inside the bait. Just fold the hook guard into position and you're all set. Weedless tubes work magic for any fish that seek thick cover, including walleye, crappies, perch, largemouth bass, and pike.

When fish are tucked tightly into cover, it's usually a sign that they are either turned right off or, at the very least, are not actively feeding. In this case, use a weedless hook and a short Carolina rig. Rigging with a short Carolina is a cinch. Just thread an appropriately sized slip sinker on your line, thread on a small bead, then tie on a small barrel swivel. Then tie on a one- to three-foot length of monofilament and your tube. When a fish hits, the line slides through the slip sinker and the fish feels no resistance. This way, it holds the bait longer, giving you more time to set the hook.

The standard for Carolina rigs is to use a heavy egg or bullet weight, ideally one made from steel or brass that makes more noise as it bangs across the bottom. But you can also rig with any slip-style sinker, including the Lindy walking style so popular with walleye anglers, or the new Lindy No Snagg sinkers, which are unbeatable over nasty tackle-grabbing bottoms.

Tuning Your Lures

Tip 75

If you want your car, truck, or outboard motor to run properly, you must keep it tuned. Well, the same thing is true for fishing lures. They have to be cared for as well. When someone plays a musical instrument that's out of tune, the songs never sound right. It's no different with fishing lures—they won't work properly if something's out of whack.

Let's look at crankbaits, for instance. You can easily tell when a crankbait is out of alignment, because it'll swerve to one side or the other when you retrieve it or troll it behind your boat. In extreme cases, it may flip right over. To bring a crankbait back into alignment, take a good look at the little metal eyelet you tie your line to at the front of the lure. At times these can be bumped off center. This may happen at the factory (it could be bumped while being inserted into the package) or it could happen while fishing, when you nudge a rock or fight your last fish. To correct the problem, simply take a pair of pliers and gently bend that metal line tie in the direction you want it to go. So, if it's wandering off to the left, gently bend the eyelet to the right (as you face the lure). Easy does it though—it doesn't take much of an adjustment at all. You're best to make a very gentle correction, then fire out a short cast and see the result. It may be fine now, or you may have to make further adjustments until it runs straight.

Inline spinners, which run on a thin wire shaft, can also be knocked out of tune by fish. Again, gentle adjustments with the pliers will bring them back into form. Years ago I used to fish a rock pile at the foot of Rondeau Bay. When the wind blew out of the west, this rock pile, which was surrounded by weeds, would often become quite muddied up, due to the wave action disturbing the bottom sediments. It held good numbers of pike and largemouth bass, even though it was only the size of two or three boats in diameter. In that muddy water, I would fish the rocks with medium-running crankbaits, literally bouncing them off the rocks.

You can intentionally bend the eye of a lure to make it veer off to the side on the retrieve—ideal for fish holding under boat docks, overhanging brush, or ice shelves.

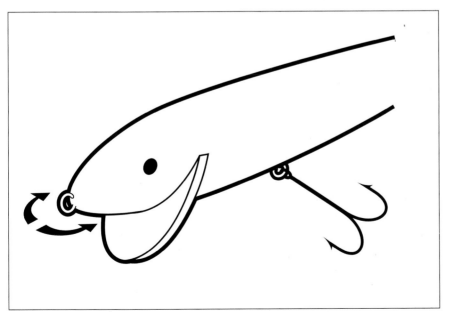

Bend the line tie to the left or right to make the lure run more to that side. Careful though! It only takes a subtle adjustment!

It doesn't take much to knock lures like spinnerbaits out of whack. Bending the arm even a little bit can affect performance.

This was the key—you had to have your lure crash into the rocks now and then, or you just wouldn't get any bites. With this type of fishing, it was very common to knock your crankbaits out of alignment, so we were constantly having to retune the baits by adjusting the front line tie with pliers.

Tuning a spinnerbait or buzzbait is even easier. All you need to do is hold the lure in front of you, as though you were sighting in a rifle, and gently twist the wire to the left or right so that it's absolutely in line with your hook. Spinnerbaits are notorious for being bent out of shape by fish, especially large pike. Over time, you have to watch because the wire can weaken from repeated bending. That's why I've become such a big fan of the new titanium wire spinnerbaits. When the folks at Strike King showed me their new titanium spinnerbait, I knew I had to have some. Titanium will bend all over the place, then snap right back to its original shape. Although these lures cost more than regular spinnerbaits, they are far more economical in the long run, besides being less fuss.

CHAPTER 5

Trout & Salmon Tips

Crankbaits for Stream Trout

Tip 76

Big trout don't get that way by eating tiny foods. You may occasionally see giant trout sipping micro-bugs off a stream surface, but to keep their weight, most trout exist on much larger prey, including smaller fish and crayfish. This is why wobbling plugs such as the Heddon Tadpolly and Rebel Crickhopper can be so deadly for big stream trout.

The best way to fish these little crankbaits, or minibaits as I like to call them, is to stand upstream of the pool and drop the bait back to the fish, using the current to impart all the action. By swinging your rod tip from side to side you can cover an entire pool this way. One trick is to bend the front line tie so that the bait veers off to one side. You can then swing your bait beneath undercut banks, overhangs, or even ice shelves to reach steelhead that wouldn't see your offering otherwise. Mark the bait with a waterproof pen so you can tell at a glance which side it runs to.

A selection of some of Bob Izumi's favorite crankbaits for trout.

This method of fishing crankbaits is basically a scaled-down version of the popular West Coast technique called "hot shotting." In a nutshell, you park your boat upstream of a promising-looking hole and use the current to slowly drift your crankbait downstream to the fish. On a smaller river you can do the same thing in waders, by simply standing upstream of a deep pool. The current gives the lure all the action it needs. It's a simple technique, and it works like magic.

Fishing Where the Fish Are

Tip 77

If you're accustomed to fishing in lakes and big rivers large enough to drive up and down in a bass boat, you will experience culture shock the first couple of times you fish in small creeks for trout or salmon. By small, I mean shallow creeks that you fish from a pair of waders, rather than from a boat.

The problem with streams is that the spots appear incredibly obvious. Big, blatant pools just about scream *Fish!*, as do deep bends and areas where there's overhanging brush. These spots can lead you astray though. This is especially true on streams that receive a fair bit of fishing pressure.

As a case in point, in southern Ontario, most streams are closed to trout fishing through the winter, with the official season opening in most places on the last Saturday in April. By then, people who have waited all winter to wet a line head out en masse, and the crowds can be very heavy, especially on popular, well-known streams. In fact, angling pressure can become so heavy that the fish sometimes abandon those big, obvious pools and move into less obvious spots, just to escape constantly being disturbed. That's when *fishing where the fish are* comes into play.

The last bit of flat water just before a calm pool spills out into a rapids is a spot most anglers miss. When fishing pressure is heavy, these one-fish spots can save the day.

It's important to realize that fish move around within a river, in response to fishing pressure. Keep your eyes open as you fish, and be prepared to try the spots everyone else seems to have overlooked. Forget the big, obvious pools and, instead, try under overhanging banks, under a protective cap of white foam behind a big rock in the middle of raging rapids, beneath streamside brush, or alongside partially submerged logs. They're definitely one-fish spots, but if you can find enough of them, you can have quite a day.

I have a couple of friends who are serious trout anglers, and they often seek out the less obvious spots. If they see a big pool, literally ringed with eager fishermen, none of whom is catching much, they'll throw a cast alongside a nondescript looking rock in the middle of a riffle. It might be a marginal place to find a fish, but more often than not, the result is the same. Presto! Fish on! The other people fishing the big pool without any bites can't believe it, and put it down to luck.

But it isn't luck at all. My friends know that when they see that big crowd of people, chances are the fish in that pool are going to be somewhat less than enthusiastic to eat a bait. So they look for places nearby where fish might sneak in order to avoid the anglers. Once these fish settle down, they're very catchable. Often the first cast tells you all you need to know. My friends also realize, though, that they won't catch big numbers of trout from any one location. Once they land the fish, it's time to move on to the next one-fish spot.

When they talk about fishing where the fish are, my friends really mean fishing where the active, receptive fish are, and that's a key difference. Although the anglers rimming the big, obvious pool may even see trout swimming around there, the fishing pressure has probably turned the fish off. So even though they're visible to the anglers, the fish probably won't hit anything.

This whole concept of ignoring fish that are obviously being pressured and, instead, targeting fish in other, secondary locations that no one else has bothered with, also applies to lake fishing. In fact, it's the basis for many tournament strategies.

Pier Fishing for Salmon

• Tip 78

If you like to catch big fish with a minimum of fuss or effort, then early autumn on the Great Lakes is truly heaven on earth. That's when you can catch really big trout and salmon from shore—no boat or fancy equipment is required. It's the easiest big-game fishing on the planet.

Great Lakes trout and salmon spend most of their life far offshore where you need a decent boat and some specialized gear to catch them. Come late summer they home in on tributary streams. Until the autumn rains raise river water levels high enough to allow fish migration, the salmon stack up off river mouths where they patiently wait. Although the fish no longer feed heavily, some may continue to snack on the odd baitfish and just about all of them can be enticed to hit a lure out of reflex, curiosity, or both. These fish are at their peak weight and physical condition, and put up epic fights, even on heavy equipment.

Most of the fish you catch will be adult chinook salmon, ranging in size from 10 to 40 pounds. Chinooks don't jump a whole lot, but few freshwater fish can peel line from your reel as quickly. Big chinooks can sustain 25 miles per hour runs for unbelievable distances.

You'll also hook the occasional brown trout—unmistakable with their flanks covered in huge black dots—which average 6 to 8 pounds but can top 30. The current Canadian record brown trout was caught by casting from shore, as were the two previous records. Notice a pattern here?

Nickel-silver steelhead are also common shoreline catches. There's no mistaking them—as soon as you hook them, steelhead are out of

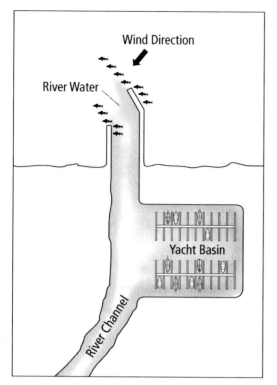

Pay attention to details when pier fishing. Most fish will be caught on the windward side of the pier. If recent rains have muddied the river water, cast where this muddy river water mixes with the clear lake water. If the two waters happen to mix on the windward side of the pier, you could be in for a bonanza!

the water in wild, cartwheeling jumps that can clear the surface by three feet.

Although you can catch these fish at any time of day, the peak action typically comes from about an hour before dusk to an hour after, and again in the morning, from just before first light until an hour or two after sunrise. This is convenient because you can fish before work and after supper. You can go every day if you like, without interrupting your normal weekday routines.

The actual fishing is dead simple—you find a pier at or near the mouth of a tributary stream used by salmon, then walk out and start casting. That's pretty much all there is to it. Salmon sniffing out the mouth of a spawning stream can and do wander just about anywhere. That said, there are three definite patterns to watch for, since they affect fish movement.

The first pattern relates to sunlight. Salmon don't have eyelids, so bright sunshine will drive them deep. When fishing in the evening, don't expect many fish to wander close to shore until the sun begins to sink on the horizon. As the sun drops, more light is reflected off the surface of the lake than absorbed into it, which is why salmon wait until the last hour or two of daylight before moving close to shore in any kind of numbers. You will often see the fish jumping and splashing on the surface just before dark.

The opposite is true in the morning. Arrive on the pier prior to dawn and you'll see or hear salmon splashing around all over the place. But as the sun climbs higher in the morning sky, you'll begin to notice less fish activity in the river mouth proper and more fish jumping farther off-shore, out of casting reach. This is why dawn and dusk are far more productive fishing times than midday. While you may catch the odd fish in midafternoon, the most consistent action comes early and late.

The second predictable salmon pattern relates to wind. The rule of thumb is that you will usually catch more fish on the side of the pier facing the wind than you will on the lee side. This is especially true with brown trout, lake trout, and steelhead, which all continue to feed heavily on bait fish. While the wind will rob you of some casting dis-tance, it also pushes the fish that much closer to shore.

The third factor controlling fish location is rain. After heavy rains have raised and clouded river water, salmon go into an upstream migra-tion mode. That's when you can forget about light intensity and wind all together, and instead concentrate on the area where the off-colored river water mixes with the clear lake. Fish moving into the river will travel along this edge.

Pier anglers need to cover water, so lures you can cast a long way work best. Spoons work well, as do heavy crankbaits such as the ½-ounce and ¾-ounce Cordell Spot.

The key isn't so much what you use as the color. Early and late in the day, plain silver or gold finishes outproduce everything else. For fishing in the dark at dawn or dusk, use the same lures but in glow-in-the-dark finishes.

Some spoons come in glow finishes straight from the factory. Others will require a touch-up with some phosphorescent paint before you head out. Illuminating this paint with a flashlight or, better yet, a camera flash makes it glow brilliant green for several minutes. In the dark water, you want to make it easy for salmon to find your bait.

You don't need box after box of lures for this kind of fishing—everything you need fits neatly into a little four-by-six pocket tackle box. Apart from the lures and a light to charge them with, the only gear you require are some needlenose pliers for unhooking fish, a flashlight so you can see what you're doing, and a long-handled net. Keep it simple. The whole works (net excluded) fits into a small side bag.

Single Eggs for Steelhead

Tip 79

After they've been in the river for a while, steelhead will shy away from spawn bags and flies. This is the time to try single eggs instead. Single eggs work for spooky fish because they're smaller, more subtle, and far more realistic than a roe bag or a clump of skeined spawn. Steelhead become accustomed to seeing single eggs drifting along in the current. That's especially true when there are a lot of spawning salmon in the stream. In fact, steelhead pig out on eggs that get washed out of nests and drift downstream in the current. Even steelhead that ignore almost every bait and lure can often be fooled with a single egg.

Single salmon eggs need to be treated in one way or another before they will stay on a hook. The simplest way to handle them is to boil them in water for a few seconds. Timing is everything here, as eggs left boiling too long will become brittle and split when you try to slip them on the hook. So keep a hook handy as you cook the eggs, so you can test them as you go. Start with a 20-second bath, haul them out, then try one on the hook. You'll know whether to give the rest more time or not.

Craig Ritchie knows steelhead gorge on single eggs. The key to fishing them is to lighten your approach for the most natural presentation possible.

As you boil the eggs you'll notice they lose their natural gold color and turn milky white. That's okay, because now they resemble eggs that have washed out of a spawning redd on their own. As trout and salmon spawn, a certain number of eggs will wash away downstream, where they quickly become free-floating snacks for other fish. Any roe will turn white on contact with water, so don't worry about the color change.

The trick to fishing single eggs is to lighten up your whole approach. Use very light, thin line that's hard for the fish to see. Use a small, fine wire hook and be sure to keep a lot of distance between your split shot and the hook—two feet at least. Otherwise, fish single eggs just like roe and you'll catch fish.

Small Stream Trouting

Tip 80

Fishing for trout in small creeks and streams is a lot of fun. It's simple fishing—no boat, simple tackle, and the spots in smaller creeks are usually fairly obvious. Plus you're usually wading in the water right with the fish in beautiful places. It's easy to get hooked on it.

The difference between good stream trout fishermen and great ones is that the best anglers pay attention to the details. Details include things such as wading slowly and not spooking the trout by kicking up mud from the bottom or splashing the water. Even when you're walking along the bank, it's important not to make too much noise and commotion, or to throw your shadow across the water. This is because most of the predators creek fish encounter are airborne ones. Trout are, therefore, conditioned to be on the lookout for any overhead movement.

Always take your time to get into the best casting position before firing out a cast, because your first opportunity is your best one. It doesn't matter whether you're fishing with baits or lures, trout in creeks are accustomed to seeing prey moving with the current. So, cast well upstream of where you actually want to fish, and let the current take your offering to the fish.

The biggest trout will, as a rule, be in the heaviest cover. One trick that I've seen good anglers use is to toss a tiny stick into the water well upstream of the place they want to fish and watch it as it drifts downstream. The stick's path reveals little current breaks that could harbor fish. These little breaks aren't always visible, even to well-trained eyes.

Key spots to try are the places where riffles flow into deep, slow pools, and again where the pools spill out to the next riffle. Fallen trees with deep water under them are always good bets, too. One of the best spots is the area directly underneath overhanging vegetation.

Overhanging trees and long grass represent both protection from overhead predators and a source of food from the insects that are always falling into the water. Spots where deep water edges up to a tall, grassy bank can be awesome later in the season, when grasshoppers are abundant. The trout snack on grasshoppers the same way you or I gobble up peanuts.

You can fish these spots with fly tackle, a light spinning outfit and little crankbaits, spinners, and jigs, or use a bait rig with a tiny hook, small split shot, and a tiny float to control your drift. The float rig is probably the most precise way to fish creeks, since you can use the float to steer the bait around obstructions and efficiently work a patch of cover.

I'll never forget one rainy morning fishing a small creek that flows into Lake Ontario with hockey legend Bobby Orr. Now, Bobby is a serious angler—he's fished for everything from creek trout to tarpon to tuna. Yet at that time, he had never tried his luck catching rainbow trout in small creeks. Because it was a rainy day, we spent a long time sitting in the Suburban, waiting for things to clear up enough before we could begin shooting a show segment. Eventually we got underway.

Using little floats and long noodle rods, we had a blast and caught a lot of rainbows. As an experienced angler, Bobby got the hang of things right away. Interestingly, Bobby would always bow to the fish when they jumped, something he had learned while tarpon fishing. Bowing is said to reduce the impact on the line, preventing break-offs or pulling the hook free. Atlantic salmon fishermen use this technique as well.

The spot we were fishing had a lot of overhead trees, and quickly enough, Bobby and I came to face another reality of small stream trout fishing. When you go to set the hook on a fish, you hope you make contact. Because if you don't, next thing you know your float, line, and everything comes rocketing out of the water and winds up snarled in one of those overhanging trees. Bobby laughed like crazy every time he or I did it. He even yelled to the camera to keep rolling, he didn't want to see it edited out. Since the TV series is called *Real Fishing* it was left in the show.

Weather and Small Stream Steelhead

• Tip 81

Talk about boom or bust! Small streams can offer incredible steelhead fishing or the absolute worst. Weather controls it all, and rain is the key. Steelhead won't enter small streams that run low and clear. To bring the fish in from the sea, rain is needed to raise the water level of

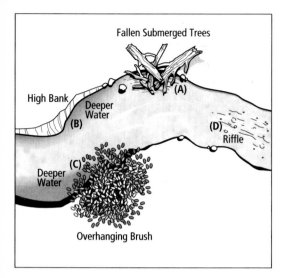

Fallen Submerged Trees

High Bank

Deeper Water

(A)

(B)

(D) Riffle

Deeper Water

(C)

Overhanging Brush

Key hiding spots for steel-head in small streams include logjams (A), deep water alongside eroded banks (B), and beneath overhanging vegetation (C). Unless steelhead are actually spawning or migrating upstream, they avoid the shallows (D), where they are most vulnerable.

the streams. Fish only enter small streams when they're running high, even though the water may be the color of chocolate milk.

Trying to catch fish in that milky water is difficult at best. The fish are there, but with the water clarity averaging four inches or less, getting them to notice your bait is tough. This is why the best fishing normally comes a day or two after the runoff peaks, as the water drops and clears to a deep green color. When the water is deep green in color, the newly arrived steelhead still feel safe, yet such water is also clear enough for them to find your bait. This prime fishing period can last anywhere from a few hours to a week, depending on the size of the stream and the type of bottom it flows over. Creeks flowing over gravel tend to clear fast, while those draining agricultural areas, or with bottoms of silt, sediment, or clay, remain off-colored for much longer.

Streams that have begun to drop and clear to that magical deep green color represent optimum conditions for steelhead fishing. Pools and runs are key spots where the fishing is often incredibly easy. You'll catch the most fish by drifting with spawn, either directly on bottom or with the aid of a sensitive float. Note that I said a sensitive float, not a small float. Upon arriving at a small stream, many anglers instinctively scale their tackle down, switching to tiny floats, light leaders, and small hooks, baits, and split shot—regardless of the water conditions. This is a big mistake.

Rule number one of steelhead fishing is that the trout will always be on bottom and so should you. Depth changes in small streams are normally far more abrupt than in bigger rivers, so being able to get your bait down deep in a hurry gives you a big advantage. You just can't do this with tiny floats and little shot, because the little weights take too long to sink. I can't count how many times I've watched anglers drifting in high water with super-fine finesse rigs, oblivious to the fact that the current is sweeping their lines downstream before the bait sinks anywhere close to the fish.

When the water runs high and green-colored, you simply don't need to use super-light lines, dust shot, micro hooks, and needle-thin floats. In fact, with a bit of color in the water, you're better off to use a slightly larger bait than normal, which is easier for the fish to see. This, in turn, demands a slightly larger hook, which needs larger shot to get it down in the current. The bigger shot demand a bigger float.

When fishing the runoff on small streams, larger gear also helps you to steer hooked fish around snags and logjams. If you don't need to use ultralight four-pound line to get hits, why handicap yourself? Go with eight-pound test instead—you'll land more fish and save tackle as well, by losing less gear to sticks and snags.

Obviously you want to make hay while the sun shines, so try to be on the water as much as possible while stream conditions are at their best. This is where knowing the character of a couple of different creeks comes into play. Because different streams clear at different rates, you can move from one river to the next as each one turns prime. Once a particular stream clears and fishing becomes tough, switch to another creek where conditions remain more favorable.

The big challenge to small stream steelheading comes once the run-off subsides and the river goes back to running low and clear. Some fish may drop back out of the creek altogether, while others will hide in logjams and deep holes. You can still catch them, but it takes a bit of stealth.

Catching steelhead in small, clear streams calls for a fundamentally different approach than most steelheaders are accustomed to. The tactics that work don't resemble what you would call "classic" trout techniques. Far from it.

First, it's important to remember that steelhead are cold-blooded animals and, in cold water, you'll find most of them in slow, deep pools. Holding in slower currents requires less energy, and all fish lose a bit of zip when they're living in ice water.

Because the fish will begin to drop back downstream as the water clears, you normally find the biggest concentrations of steelhead in the lower reaches of small streams. While you may find isolated pockets of fish here and there along the river, those first half-dozen pools upstream from the lake are the ones you really want to fish hard. On most streams, these are the wide, featureless-looking ones with little current, tons of logs, and possibly even banks lined with cattails. It may feel a bit strange fishing in these slow, marshy pools, but that's where the fish are.

Low, clear water is where you do want to haul out those little bobbers, light lines, tiny hooks, and all the finesse gear. In the slow current and super clear water, you will get more hits by fishing small baits on thin four-pound monofilament. Small baits, in turn, demand small hooks, shot, and floats.

Floats are pretty much standard fare when fishing slow pools in clear conditions. You can catch fish by drifting on bottom, but in the gentle current you will have a tough time keeping your bait moving along naturally without the aid of a float. In the lower reaches of most streams, the bottom is normally littered with snags, giving you all the more incentive to keep your bait slightly off of it.

When fishing clear water, it's almost always best to avoid wading at all costs. Keep back from the bank and try to stay low, to avoid spook-ing fish. Some anglers go so far as to wear camouflaged hunting jackets, which is sensible thinking. In low, clear water, the fish will almost always see you before you see them. Then it's too late.

One good tactic is to use cover along the bank to hide your approach. Instead of walking up to the river edge, approach the fish from behind some trees. Use streamside cover to help hide you from the fish.

Fishing clear water effectively calls for long, accurate casts. You will need to put your rig right on the money, sometimes from considerable distances. Learning to do so, while keeping your line away from over-hanging branches and such, definitely takes practice. Long rods make it easier to pendulum your rig into position.

Some of the better spots include logjams, deep bend pools, any steep bank areas, or right along the edge of cattail beds. Cattails are often hollow underneath, and steelhead will sit right in them. Big patches of floating leaves and debris can also produce fish if they float over deep water. Even clumps of weeds on bottom can hold steelhead. You may begin to feel like you're fishing for largemouth bass, but the truth is, in small streams, steelhead behave far more like largemouth than most anglers imagine.

The good news is that, if you rig up correctly, approach quietly, and make a good presentation, you'll catch steelhead. You'll also have all the fish to yourself, which may be the biggest benefit to fishing small streams.

Worms for Trout

Tip 82

Worms are almost the perfect trout bait, and, if you're willing to spend an hour or two searching the lawn with a flashlight, they're truly inex-pensive. They are certainly easy to transport and care for. They are also versatile—you can fish them 100 different ways. And, perhaps most important, trout eat worms like candy. What more could you ask for? So, just in time for spring trout fishing, here's the quick and dirty on Mother Nature's best trout bait.

When worm fishing for trout, you have to match the size of the bait to the size of the fish you expect to catch. Be realistic. If most of the fish in the stream weigh a pound or less, you'll do far better with small worms than you will with python-sized night crawlers. But if it's the big guys you're after, or if you're thinking steelhead, more meat is the way to go.

If you need small worms, you certainly can break bigger ones in half. But they won't work nearly as well. For starters, worm parts die quickly. They also look too thick for their length and don't move the same way as complete worms. It's better to use the small but complete worms, if you have the choice. Bait dealers often sell smaller worms as "trout worms," with usually 50 or so to a container. For most trout fishing, they're your best bet.

The opposite end of the scale applies when you're gunning for a four-pound or better trout or steelhead. These big fish put on muscle by eating big stuff. Worms that look like brown garter snakes are just the ticket—the bigger the better.

Small hooks, thin, light lines, and simple rigging are best when fishing worms for stream trout.

The simplest approach is a single, small hook stuck once through the collar or through the tail end of the worm. Balling worms up on the hook may be a good idea when dealing with perch and sunfish, but trout won't hesitate to suck in the whole thing, so there's no benefit. And by hooking the worm over and over again into a ball, you kill its natural appearance. Better to just hook it once and let it wriggle as Mother Nature intended.

The reason for hooking through the collar is that it's the toughest part of a worm's soft skin—you're less likely to rip it off on a cast. Some anglers prefer to hook worms once through the nose, reducing the chance of the worm wrapping on the hook. I prefer to poke it once through the tail, which eliminates the chance of piercing the worm's primitive heart and killing it. Remember dissecting a worm back in high school science class? There's lots of stuff up front you can damage. Hook it in the rump end and it will last for hours.

It goes without saying that this fine, finesse approach doesn't work if you tie the hook to some heavy line that looks like anchor rope. Use fine four- or six-pound test for a stealthy presentation, especially in clear water.

By far the best time to fish worms is the day after a spring shower. Rains push worms to the ground surface, so it's common for trout to see them immediately following a rain. Rains also wash all sorts of bugs and other critters into streams, setting up a nice flow of free food, putting trout in a super-receptive mood. Rain also tends to color the water a bit, so spooky trophy trout are comfortable moving out of their brushy lairs and situating themselves in the current, where they can take advantage of the feeding opportunity. This also puts them in a place where trout anglers can reach them. It's tough to drift a bait into the spots where these bigger fish normally live, such as under overhanging banks or deep into wood piles. Best to fish for them when they're out in the open.

Make a point of being on the water the very next day after a good spring rain. Phone in sick if you have to (luckily I'm not in that situation). Being on the stream four days after a rain just isn't the same. You have to be there before the water drops and clears. If you're there when you should be, the exact time of day won't matter one bit because the slightly colored water will keep trout active right through the afternoon. It's not a great-action-at-first-light-and-nothing-since deal.

Look for trout to sit right in the current. The best spot is the upstream end of deep holding pools—right where the fast water ends. You'll also find feeding trout in shallow riffles, especially those near high stream banks or those with lots of logs or big rocks breaking up the flow. Anywhere that trout can dash out to pick off a snack drifting by in the current yet still find protection from predators is worth checking out.

Yarn Flies

Tip 83

If you polled steelhead anglers from the Great Lakes or West Coast for their favorite baits or lures, my guess is salmon or trout eggs would head the list. But, for first-time steelheaders, this choice creates an obvious dilemma. After all, you've got to catch a fish before you can harvest some eggs. Also, many people don't like messing around with fish eggs. So what's the solution?

Yarn flies, of course. Nothing more than an inch of yarn held to a small, single hook by the knot to your fishing line, yarn flies are incredibly simple yet, in the right situations, perhaps even more effective than real roe.

Yarn flies work best in places such as the heads or tails of pools, in deep fast runs, or in any other place where steelhead just don't have time to closely examine a bait before it's swept away by the current. In these spots, steelhead must decide to hit by appearances alone. Because you control the size and color of the yarn, you can tailor your yarn flies for use in low and clear or high and off-colored conditions. That's why so many veteran steelheaders carry a wide variety of yarn in their vests at all times.

Because yarn is slightly buoyant, it floats up somewhat in the current, drifting along at eye level to the fish, where they can easily spot it. And because it collapses when they eat it, yarn is a great bait in terms of hook-up percentages. In fact, it's quite common for steelhead to get the yarn caught in their teeth, giving you lots of time to set the hook.

Yarn flies aren't just a great steelhead bait. They also work well for resident stream trout that eat roe, as well as migratory brown trout, coho, and chinook salmon, and even walleye—especially when used in conjunction with bait. Next time you're heading out for a day of steelhead fishing and you don't have any real roe, try using yarn flies and you might be shocked at how well they work.

CHAPTER 6

Bass Tips

Competitive Instincts

Tip 84

Fish are highly competitive creatures. For instance, imagine you're sitting on a dock and you see five or six little bass over the side. If you were to drop a small piece of worm into the water, chances are that all of the little bass would make a beeline for it. Now, when one of them grabs the worm, watch closely to see what it does next. Because you can almost guarantee that it'll try to swim away from the others with the worm dangling from its mouth.

Just as likely, those other five or six bass are not going to take this sitting down. They're going to chase after the one with the worm and try to steal it away. That's what I mean by competitive instinct, and it can be an angler's best friend.

Even though we're talking about juvenile bass, the very same principle applies to just about every other species of fish. Despite what most anglers think, life's not a bowl of cherries below the surface of the water. So, when food is at stake, it's every man, or perhaps I should say fish, for himself.

If your friend hooks onto a fair-sized bass, don't be afraid to throw a cast right beside his lure, even while he's still fighting the fish. Because you never know how many other fish are chasing after his lure, looking for an easy meal to steal. It's amazing how many fish you can catch this way, especially when fishing for schooling species.

You can tap into competitive instincts in other ways too. Over the years I've fished with literally hundreds if not thousands of people, and it's amazing how many anglers simply don't pay attention to the water behind their lure as they're finishing a retrieve. Countless times in filming the TV show, when fun fishing, or in fishing tournaments, I've had fish follow my lure. They're interested but not convinced just yet. And the way to make them hit is to play on that competitive instinct.

I'm talking about trout, walleye, bass, pike, muskie, and a variety of saltwater species. Many times when a fish is interested in your lure, half the battle is already won, because you can turn an interested fish into a caught fish just by keeping your eyes open and looking. Many times a following fish will spook once it sees either you or the boat or something that just doesn't seem right. But if you pay attention and keep that lure in the water as that fish is approaching, you can often catch it.

Sometimes you can trigger a strike by slightly changing the lure's direction. For instance, if you see a fish following your bait, try suddenly swinging your rod right or left and changing the direction of your lure. Another thing that can instigate strikes is a change in speed, such as slowing down, maybe even stopping the lure, or killing it so that it either suspends or floats up to the surface or sinks down to the bottom.

A number of years ago my brother Wayne and I were fishing a Pro Bass tournament on southern Ontario's Rice Lake. We decided to fish the Otonabee River early in the morning with some topwater lures. I was using a Rebel Pop-R and had a smallmouth grab it. As I was fighting it to the boat, suddenly it got a little heavier than I thought it should have been. When I looked I saw a muskie clamped right around the side of my bass. It wasn't a large muskie, probably about 15 pounds or so, but obviously the bass I was reeling in was the perfect size for dinner. Finally it let go and I got the bass into the boat. It was a keeper, so I put it in the livewell. Luckily it had only a light, horseshoe-shaped row of teeth marks around its back, but it was still alive, and, I think, well. Wayne and I looked down and saw the muskie still sitting there about two feet under the surface, in the clear water of the river. It was probably five feet from the front of the boat. Poor guy was probably waiting for me to release the bass, and I felt badly robbing him of a meal. As we're unhooking the bass and getting it into the livewell, all of a sudden we feel something hit the boat hard, and we turn to see the electric motor shaking in its mount. We ran to the front of the boat, looked over the bow and, lo and behold, that muskie had actually hit the propeller of the electric motor. It sat there, about three feet away, suspended in the water, stunned, with a little patch of ripped jaw tissue hanging from the corner of its mouth.

It goes to show you that some of these following fish are quite aggressive and can be caught. I'm certain that muskie would have hit anything we dropped in front of it. Of course, we were in a bass tournament at the time. Had we been muskie fishing I'm sure we'd never have had a stupid muskie like that come to the boat. I wonder if you can rig an electric motor prop as a muskie lure? Hmmm...you never know!

Deadsticking

It sounds gruesome, but deadsticking is actually the name for a great fishing technique. As it suggests, in deadsticking you cast out your bait and then do absolutely nothing—you let it sit there like something that died. Many types of game fish are at least part-time scavengers, especially big ones that just can't let an easy meal go by.

Deadsticking works with a variety of lures, but it's at its best with lures you can work in a stop-and-go pattern, such as jigs, plastic worms, and topwaters. In fact, I'd say deadsticking has become one of my favorite ways of fishing topwater baits. The reason is simple— some of my most memorable surface catches have come on lures left sitting motionless.

One of my favorite fishing memories involves deadsticking a Heddon Zara Spook surface lure while competing in the Kenora Bass International Tournament in northwestern Ontario's Sunset Country several years ago. My friend John Vandivier and I already had a decent limit in the livewell and I was getting hungry, so we pulled in behind a point on the end of a small island. I asked John if he wanted a sandwich and cast out my Zara Spook.

You have to realize that the most popular size of Zara Spook is almost five inches long. It's a big bait. Normally you work it in a stop-and-go pattern by twitching your rod tip as you reel. It's called "Walking the Dog," and it's a proven technique for catching big bass, pike, and muskie.

I cast the Zara out as far as I could with my baitcasting outfit, which would have been 80 to 100 feet. Since we'd stopped for lunch, I put my rod down and headed for the cooler. Keep in mind, when we're tournament fishing we have at least 25 to 35 rods scattered about in the boat. Legally you can only use one line at a time per angler, but in this case we'd been fishing a number of techniques over the course of the day, so there were lots of rods in the boat sticking out in every direction. The boat looked like a big, fiberglass porcupine.

As I reached into the cooler to grab some food, I heard this enormous splash—I mean a huge commotion—as if someone had thrown a building block into the water. Because my head was in the cooler and I couldn't see, I assumed John was still casting and yelled for him to set the hook. Imagine my surprise when I looked up and saw John still working his bait and not fighting a fish.

I scrambled to the front of the boat and looked at this huge maze of rods piled every which way. Finally I figured out which rod I'd cast out, grabbed it, reeled up the slack line, and was amazed to find the bass had hooked itself. It turned out to be the biggest bass we caught during the entire tournament, and it came on a Zara Spook sitting dead in the water for over a minute doing nothing.

Deadsticking reminds me of playing with our cat. You know, where you take a ball of wool, peel off a couple of feet of loose material, and twitch it along the floor while the cat chases after it. All of a sudden you stop moving the wool and the cat also stops, dead in its path, just sitting there staring at it. Eventually that cat just can't stand it anymore and jumps the wool anyway.

That's what I feel deadsticking is in fishing. It's a technique that drives large fish crazy because they're waiting for the bait to move and it just sits there, defiantly. It's a battle of nerves, and the mindless plastic lure always seems to win. Who says curiosity only got the cat?

Details on Docks

Tip 86

One of the most important things to consider when you're looking for fish is cover. By cover, I mean things such as weedbeds, boulders, and fallen trees—features in the water that provide shelter and hiding spots for fish.

Good cover can also be man-made, and of this variety, there isn't any better than boat docks. In fact, oodles of bass tournaments have been won fishing boat docks.

But you know, as good as they can be, when there are hundreds or even thousands of docks fringing the shoreline, you've got to be able to quickly pick out the docks that are going to produce fish and the ones that will draw blanks. Fortunately, after you've looked at them for a while, the best docks are easy to spot, because they share a number of common characteristics.

Good docks sit low on the water, have large cribbing or supports, and have plenty of lead-in cover. Poor docks sit high in the water, have skinny supports, and lack lead-in cover such as weeds.

For example, the best docks are usually built on wooden posts and small rock-filled cribs, as opposed to being free-floating structures or structures built on thin metal posts. And docks hanging low to the water almost always seem to attract better fish than those perched high above the surface.

Good Dock

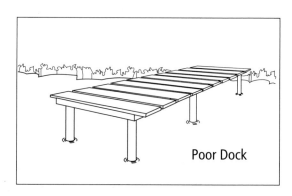

Poor Dock

I like docks that are long and wide, and that shade as much water as possible. Even better are those built over some form of natural structure or cover, such as a dock that covers a pile of boulders, or one that overtops a drop-off or break line.

Another great feature to look for, and one I've used to win many tournaments over the years, is outboard motor scours. Outboard motors have a tendency to scour craterlike holes out of soft bottoms, right where the motor is positioned when the boat is docked. Most people park their boat in the same position each time out. When they come out and fire up their outboard motor, then slip it into reverse gear, it erodes a little patch of bottom. Over time that little patch can become a pretty big hole—large enough to conceal a bass or two. In shallow water, this can be a key spot holding fish.

A quiet approach is essential when fishing docks and boathouses.

If you're going to fish docks, you have to be polite and courteous. If you accidentally get snagged on some guy's mooring rope, make a special effort to get your hook out of there. Don't leave your worm hooks or jigs or tube jigs stuck in their property. Never forget that people swim around docks.

If people are using their dock, go around them with the electric motor and give them lots of space. Do not, under any circumstances, fish a dock that's in use—unless, of course, the people have expressly invited you to do so.

At a recent Pro Bass Classic I decided to fish a little stretch of docks on a heavily populated lake in southern Ontario. I proceeded to catch two good bass under one dock when I noticed this water-skiing boat coming at me. At the last minute the boat turned, and this daredevil skier came right at the bow of my boat, completely soaking me in water. He missed hitting my electric motor by about three feet. It turned out their dock was a few cottages down the lake from where I was, and they didn't want me to fish there.

To this day I cannot believe this lunatic risked his life to get me soaked, but the next time I see a skier coming at me when I'm fishing I guarantee my seven-and-a-half-foot flipping rod is going to be at a right angle to the boat, facing in his direction. Remember to respect people's property when fishing, but other people should show some respect to you, too. It has to be a two-way street.

The South Western Ontario Bass Association (SWOBA) had their classic at my old home stomping grounds, Rondeau Bay, one year back in the late 1980s. John Vandivier and I had a great year fishing their circuit, winning two out of the three qualifying tournaments prior to the year-end classic. We already had a limit of bass in the boat, but as the day was winding down, we came alongside a line of docks. I told John that I'd never fished this row of docks and wanted to give it a try. I'll never forget the people on shore waving to us, enjoying the summer weekend, having a few refreshments. I flipped under a dock, felt a hit, set the hook, and missed it. John flipped right in behind me, felt a hit, set the hook, and caught this three-pound bass. We put it in the livewell, picked out the smallest fish, and released it right there. The folks on the dock were cheering for us.

I looked at my watch and told John we had to rock and roll because we were running out of time. We gave ourselves about 10 minutes to make a seven-mile run back to the weigh-in for the final day of this two-day event. Needless to say, that bass from the boat docks helped us win the SWOBA Classic title and a fully rigged bass boat. That was a more enjoyable experience than getting soaked by the kamikaze water-skier.

Tip 87 · Flipping and Pitching

For more than 25 years I've enjoyed fishing competitive tournaments for largemouth bass. And, most of all, I love fishing for them in very heavy cover. I learned a long time ago that the best largemouth are usually the ones tucked into the thickest cover. They're also the fish that see the fewest anglers over the course of a year. The heavy cover makes many lures and presentations virtually useless. To catch these fish, you have to pitch and flip.

Flipping, a style of fishing developed in California, is a great way of carefully fishing very heavy cover. You need a long, seven-and-a-half-foot, heavy-action flipping rod with anywhere from 17- to 20-pound test, and a baitcasting reel. Strip some line off the reel, say about 7 to 10 feet, hold it in your hand, and using an underhand pendulum motion, swing the bait (or "flip" it) into small, open pockets in the heavy cover. Drop your rod tip as the lure, normally a plastic worm or a jig, sinks to the bottom, watching the line for movement that would indicate a bite. That's all there is to it.

You can flip on the edges of the lily pads, right in the middle of them, on the edges of fallen trees, or right into the tree's branches. You can flip in just about any cover imaginable.

The idea of the heavy equipment, by the way, is to haul the fish out of the cover. You might feel that a super-powerful rod and 25-pound line is overkill for bass that average two to three pounds apiece, but you won't feel that way once you hook a fish and have to haul it out of thick cover. It isn't easy, and it's often out of the question with lighter equipment.

The key to successful flipping is to be super-quiet. Some of these spots can be only six inches deep, and the bass can be extremely wary. A quiet approach is essential.

You want to pitch the outside edge of the cover first, just in case any fish are poking about the edges. If the wind is blowing, start fishing on the windiest side, then progressively work in toward the middle.

Pitching is similar to flipping, but it works at a longer range. For most flipping you're usually within 15 feet of your spot, sometimes much less. But with pitching you can stay back 20, maybe 40 feet, to avoid spooking fish with the boat. You use the same underhand pendulum motion to get your lure into the spot, but rather than holding the slack line in your hand, releasing it at the appropriate moment to send your lure on its way to the target, you pitch off the reel, making a gentle, underhand lob. The idea is to have your lure travel very close to the water's surface so that it makes the least splash or disturbance possible when it finally lands. A straight overhead cast can make too much noise, crashing the lure into the water hard and sending the fish scurrying for cover.

Pitching is perfect for coaxing lunker largemouth from heavy cover.

I prefer a seven-and-a-half-foot flipping stick for pitching, because I like the added leverage it provides.

It takes a bit of practice to get the hang of pitching and flipping. Practicing with a target helps, but there's no substitute for on-the-water experience. Be patient and it will come to you soon enough.

One common mistake when you're just starting out with flipping and pitching is not getting your reel engaged quickly enough. Many times when you're flipping and pitching an area and the fish are active and grabbing your bait immediately, you can miss fish by not being ready to set the hook when the lure lands on the water's surface. Setting the hook with the free spool still disengaged will cause a huge backlash—trust me on this!

When you flip your lure into the cover, it's best that you lower your rod tip as the lure hits the water, so that it sinks vertically down into the cover. If you don't, you're defeating the whole purpose. When the lure hits the water on a tight line, it will swing like a pendulum back toward you and away from the fish. Making sure it hits the water on a controlled, slack line will allow it to sink straight down, and hopefully, into the jaws of a trophy bass.

It may seem obvious, but the best lures for flipping and pitching are weedless. Flipping jigs, tipped with either a pork or a soft plastic trailer, are the most popular choice. But don't overlook traditional soft plastic worms, rigged Texas-style, with the sinker pegged firmly into position at the worm's nose. Soft plastic lizards and crayfish are also extremely productive baits for flipping and pitching—especially on lakes that have a lot of angling pressure. Once again, they're just a little different from what most people use, so they're often new to the fish.

How to Peg a Sinker

When people fish a plastic worm, they usually put a free-sliding, bullet-shaped sinker just ahead of the lure. The principle, of course, is that when a bass picks up the worm and runs off with it, the fishing line slides freely through the sinker and the fish doesn't feel any weight or resistance. But there are other times when you don't want your sinker to slide.

If you were dragging a conventional sliding sinker and worm rig through submerged tree branches, for instance, your worm would be constantly hanging over one side of the branch while your sinker was draped over the other. And, if a bass inhaled your bait, it would be difficult for you to feel or detect the strike.

So, instead, anchor the sinker in one place to stop it from sliding, making the rig resemble a jig and worm. Now, the way you actually peg it in place is really quite simple.

Once your bullet sinker is on the line, slide it down so that the base of the weight is right beside the knot holding your hook on the line. Then, jam a toothpick firmly up into the hole where the line comes through the back of the sinker and snap off the excess, jamming the sinker in place. Now, simply thread on the plastic worm as you would normally. The weight is now snuggled up against the head of the worm.

Another way of pegging a sinker in place was shown to me by Craig Ritchie. Craig simply threads a neoprene bobber stop onto his line ahead of the slip sinker. Then, he just ties on the hook, slides the sinker down to the hook, and then slides the neoprene bobber stop down the line to snug it in place.

Maybe the easiest way to peg a sinker in place is simply to buy a locking sinker. Some varieties of slip sinkers include a little wire screw in their base, sort of like a little miniature corkscrew. You just slide the sinker down to the head of the plastic worm as you would normally, then screw it into place.

My best year of tournament fishing so far was in 1995. I won the triple crown, consisting of the GM Mariner Pro Bass Classic, the GM

Mariner Pro Bass Canadian Open, and the GM Mariner Angler of the Year award, which was as good as it gets in Canadian competitive fishing for me. A number of the largemouth I caught in tournaments that year came by pegging ⅜-ounce worm sinkers up against a black and blue, four-inch, soft plastic crayfish called a Riverside Big Claw.

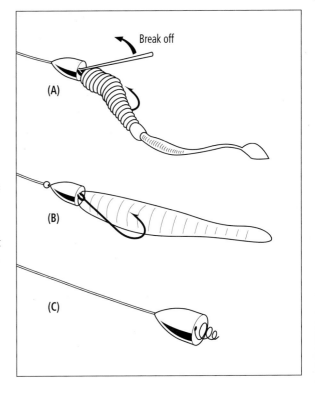

To peg a sinker, first, break off a toothpick where the sinker meets the hook (A); then either use a bobber stop to hold it snug (B) or use a screw-in sinker (C).

Some of the key fish I caught during the Canadian Open and the Classic that year were caught in heavy cover, such as lily pads, reeds, and floating mats of weeds that were blown up against the standing vegetation. Some of the matted weeds were more than six inches thick. I had to use a technique I don't really talk about much, even today, amongst some of my tournament buddies.

Many people go around big weed mats such as these and fish the edges of them. I used a different approach. I threw a pegged Big Claw or a plastic worm up in the air over the weeds with a seven-and-a-half-foot, heavy-action flipping outfit with 20- or 25-pound test line. Once the heavily weighted Big Claw swung high in the air, I flicked my rod tip down sharply, causing the lure to shoot straight down as if it were coming out of a rifle. The lure landed with such force that the bullet weight plowed through the weeds and sunk into the clear water beneath them. Many of the bass in this heavy cover weren't pressured by other anglers.

On occasion I've noticed other people attempting this method without much success. Timing is everything. If you don't flick the rod tip down hard, the lure will just fall flat right on top of the weed mat and sit there. You need to give it a good, sharp flick to drive it down through the heavy weeds.

Once it goes through the weed mat and into the clear water below, I just let it sink down to the bottom and let it sit there for about five seconds. If I don't feel any weight on it, I'll lift the bait up a few inches and then drop it again and let it sit some more.

But I've already shared enough information on this secret technique. It's deadly! Seriously, though, there are times when pegging your sinker in place has its benefits. Next time you're on the water, give it a try.

Plastic Worms

Tip 89

Plastic worms probably catch more largemouth bass every year than all other artificial lures combined. So bass anglers should rely on plastic worms for two simple reasons—they're versatile and they work.

Yet, because of this versatility, they can cause problems for some anglers. What type do you use for fishing in reeds? When is a worm too big or too small for the situation? What about color, tail shape, and hook size?

One of the most important factors about worms is their feel. Worms used to be rigid and stiff, and much too hard. Today's baits are super soft and mushy. When a largemouth bass inhales one of these soft, gooey imitations, it probably feels and tastes as good as bubble gum.

Having a bass gum your worm and hang onto it for that extra split second or two can be extremely important, because they rarely wallop a worm like they do a fast-moving crankbait or spinnerbait. Instead they inhale it, chew on it for a moment, and then spit it out. And the longer you can get a bass to hold onto your worm because it feels good, the better your chances of hooking it.

But there are times when a slightly firmer worm is a better choice. We use a harder one, for example, when we're fishing in extra heavy cover. It doesn't matter if you're casting, flipping, or pitching a worm through thick reeds, heavy weeds, or brush piles. In that kind of cover, a super soft Texas-rigged worm can easily tear or slide down your hook, whereas a slightly firmer one will come through, none the worse for wear.

Some days you can do no wrong. Bob Izumi is all smiles, holding one of two giant bass caught while fishing in Cuba with CFL veteran Blaine Schmidt.

Soft plastic baits probably have accounted for almost half the bass tournament fish I've caught over the years, because of their incredible versatility. I can work them slow, medium, or fast, in cover, out of cover, weedless, or non-weedless. They're a great finesse bait, or you can use giant worms and be a little more aggressive. By giant, I mean up to a foot long.

One of the most popular lures for largemouth bass in Cuba is a 9- to 12-inch black plastic worm. Most anglers would think this a very large worm, but even in my home province of Ontario, at the northernmost limits of the largemouth's range, the foot-longs work extremely well.

I caught my biggest bass ever on a plastic worm. It was in Cuba, where I was fishing with Canadian Football League veteran Blaine

Schmidt. We were fishing this beautiful lake in the mountains, going down a rocky shoreline that had the odd piece of wood here and there. We were throwing the worms up against the rock bank and swimming them down the drop-off, working the break along the shoreline. I caught an 11.5-pounder—needless to say, I was elated.

We'd both been fishing from the front of the boat, but, just the way it worked out, I'd been casting first. With my big bass safely landed, and me on cloud nine, I switched spots with Blaine so he could have first crack at the different spots. I wanted him to get a big fish, too.

As luck would have it, about 15 minutes later, I felt a little tap-tap on my worm, set the hook hard, and eventually landed a nine-pound largemouth. I didn't say anything, neither did Blaine, though he did give me a funny look. What can I say? Luck of the draw. I'm just glad he has a sense of humor, since we were using basically identical setups. It was an evening I'll never forget.

Rocks and Smallmouth Bass

Tip 90

Sometimes fishermen generalize so much that the point they're trying to make becomes almost meaningless. Take the case of smallmouth bass. If you ask a dozen fishermen to name the best place in a lake or river to locate smallies, the answer will invariably come back, "Near rocks."

But really, what does this mean? On most good smallmouth lakes, the entire shoreline is rocky! And, if you tried to fish all the different rock types on one of these lakes, you'd spend plenty of time fishing unproductive habitat.

So the point is this, where smallmouth bass are concerned, there are rocks, and then there are ROCKS. But before we discuss the best rock types, let's set the stage by pointing out a few kinds that generally won't harbor any appreciable number of smallies.

The best type of rocky structure for smallmouth has stones of various sizes, rather than expansive areas where all the rocks are uniform.

Well, first and foremost, there's sheet rock. That's the stuff that's found all over the Canadian north country—the typical Canadian Shield slab of granite. And while it's pretty to look at, these huge flat sheets of bedrock, as smooth as a baby's bottom, are poor spots to locate smallmouth.

Another inferior option is a rocky slope that looks like it's paved with cobblestones or small rocks all about the same size. Many people mistake these areas for prime smallmouth habitat and, after an hour or two of casting, shake their heads wondering where all the fish are.

Actually, this is the perfect lead-in to describe the kind of rocks that smallmouth *do* favor. Good smallmouth territory has everything from big boulders the size of kitchen tables to smaller rocks and stones the size of pumpkins, grapefruits, apples, and oranges. And for good measure, add gravel and coarse sand.

Watch the bottom or pay attention to your sonar when searching for shoals, reefs, or saddles. You're looking for rocks ranging from the size of a toaster to as large as a small car.

Keep in mind that when smallmouth are using rocks, they're often continuously grazing through. It's like looking at an open pasture with a bunch of grazing cattle down in one corner. That's where they are now. Later in the day, they're somewhere else. Smallmouth and rocks are the same way. You have to be there at the right time.

I think of this each summer when I fish in the Kenora Bass International Tournament, on northwestern Ontario's Lake of the Woods. Over the years my partners and I have fished a number of good rock areas for smallmouth. It's quite common to go to a great-looking rock hump or point, or rock island or saddle, and catch nothing—not a touch. Then, when you return to it a couple of hours later, you catch three or four good bass. I believe the fish simply moved through this area and were grazing like cattle.

When you're fishing smallmouth on the rocks, and you've got a known hot spot, it's a good idea to hit it continually at different times of the day so that eventually you can intercept these fish as they move through. At times it's feast, at other times it's famine.

Walking the Dog

Tip 91

Over the years, those who've watched my TV show, read my magazine, or attended any of my seminars have probably heard me refer to "walking the dog." Of course, I'm talking about a way to retrieve certain types of surface lures.

For starters, you have to realize you can't use this retrieve with just any surface bait. It must be a stick bait, such as the famous Zara Spook, or the new Spit'n Image. Now, remember that stick baits are shaped like broom handles. They have absolutely no action of their own. This is something you have to provide, and this is where walking the dog comes in.

To best explain this retrieve, let's say you've cast out a stick bait and it's sitting on the surface. The first thing to do is absolutely nothing. Just let that lure lie still on the surface until all the rings have washed away. And imagine a fish staring up at it, wondering what to do next.

Now, to retrieve it properly, some people like to position their rod tips at about 8 o'clock, while others prefer 10 o'clock. Try them both and see which you like better.

When you've decided, slowly start to reel in your line. As you do, start twitching your rod tip up and down and watch your lure. When you get the hang of it, your stick bait will swerve off first to one side, then to the other. And when you really get that dog walking, it'll march right across the surface like a toy soldier. It's a great action because it creates disturbance and calls attention to your lure, yet doesn't make a lot of noise that might spook fish in very shallow water. It's also a fairly quick way of working a topwater lure, allowing you to cover more water over the course of a day than you might be able to otherwise.

Walking the dog is a great technique for pike, muskie, and especially bass. My brother Wayne and I were fishing a team tournament on Big Rideau Lake near Ottawa one year, and our strategy was to try and catch some fish early each morning using topwater lures. We decided to fish as many points and saddles between islands as we could before the sun came up high and the fish retreated to more shaded areas. I went with a tried-and-true Zara Spook.

This dog's a retriever! Bob Izumi walked the dog with a Heddon Zara Spook and caught two bass at once—a largemouth on one hook, and a smallmouth on the other.

I got kind of a funny hit, almost like a slap on the bait, and then there was some commotion under it. I let the bait disappear, as you have to when you're surface fishing, and as it went under, I set the hook and kept constant pressure on the fish. As I got the bait near the boat I noticed there was a smallmouth bass on one of the treble hooks, and a largemouth bass on the other. Obviously both fish decided they wanted the bait at the same time. Talk about inspiring confidence!

Unfortunately the smallmouth wasn't long enough to keep, but the largemouth was. So, I put it in the livewell.

I don't remember much about the rest of the day. It's pretty rare to catch two fish on the same lure at the same time, much less two different species.

I've walked the dog for all sorts of fish in all sorts of places, usually with some success. It doesn't take long to learn how to do it right, and it's a great technique. If you're a fan of topwater fishing, it's definitely one trick you want to have in your back pocket. I can't guarantee you'll start catching fish two at a time, but I can tell you it really works.

CHAPTER 7

Pike & Muskie Tips

Figure Eight

Tip 92

One of the most exciting moments in all of fishing is when, from out of nowhere, a huge fish cruises in behind your lure, your heart skips a beat, and you may even think you hear the theme song from *Jaws*. You pray out loud, "If only that fish'll hit." Sometimes the fish does, but wishing for a bite isn't as dependable as using the good old "figure eight."

A figure eight is not some mystical gesture to the Fishing Gods. Instead, it's a special retrieve you should use when fish are following closely behind your lure. And when it works, it produces some exciting, hair-raising action.

The key to putting it into effect is to never slow down your retrieve, once you've spotted a trailing fish. In fact, try picking up the speed just a tad to give the impression your lure has been detected and is trying to escape.

Now, as your lure approaches the boat, keep reeling and, at the same time, dip your rod right into the water. Continue reeling until your leader is up next to the tip, or there's about a rod-length of line between your rod and the lure. At this point, grab your fishing rod with both hands and swish your lure in wide "figure eight" patterns, three or four feet deep, alongside the boat.

Just don't slow down your lure, even if you lose sight of the fish. And don't vary the depth. The only time to do this is when the trailing fish makes a move to close in on your bait.

Then, as you start another figure eight, bring your lure right up and over the fish's head. And plant your feet squarely, because any minute now, the fun's about to begin.

My *Real Fishing Radio Show* cohost, Gord Pyzer, catches world-class muskies each year in northwestern Ontario, and he's the biggest fan of the figure eight I know. A number of years ago, Gord and I were out videotaping in the fall and we went to one of his many small hot spots. Gord and other muskie anglers I've fished with over the years have told me to always watch behind your lure as you're bringing it to the boat. While on this outing we were using jerkbaits, and as we worked these jerkbaits over a rock point, I noticed a big shadow. As I kneeled down and poked my rod tip in the water, I began to figure eight the muskie.

This muskie was quite big—30 pounds, maybe more. Next thing you know this muskie opens its mouth and clamps down on the bait, and I proceed to set the hook what I thought was hard. My rod bends and all of a sudden the muskie opens its mouth, spits the bait out, and swims away. Needless to say the adrenaline was running, but I was also disappointed.

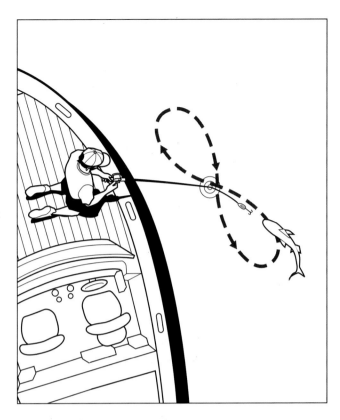

When a muskie follows your lure without biting, work your bait in a big circle or in a figure eight at boatside. Sometimes the fish will bit.

About 20 minutes later Gord says, "Let's go try that spot again." So here we are back on the same spot and I'm 99.9 percent sure it's the same muskie following the boat. I start to go into a figure eight, it opens its mouth and, once again, eats the giant wooden jerkbait. I set the hook as hard as I can, and bingo, the fish opens its mouth and swims away.

To miss the same muskie twice in a half-hour period was probably better than catching that fish. Sure, it would have been fun to catch it. But being able to look back at the experience—getting the hit, blowing it, and wishing for a second chance, then actually getting another crack at the fish and missing it again—these are the kind of memories you never forget.

Big muskie have strong jaws and impressive dental work. When they grab a big wooden lure like a jerkbait, they often sink their teeth into it. It takes incredible force to set the hooks properly. At least, that's my excuse, and I'm sticking to it.

Make Your Own Leaders

I love fishing for muskie and big northern pike. Given the teeth both these fish possess, steel leaders are an absolute must. But heavy wire leaders can impair the action of some topwater baits. They're also tough to use if you want to try fly fishing for these fish in shallow water. The answer is to make your own fine wire leaders. It's simpler to do this than you might imagine.

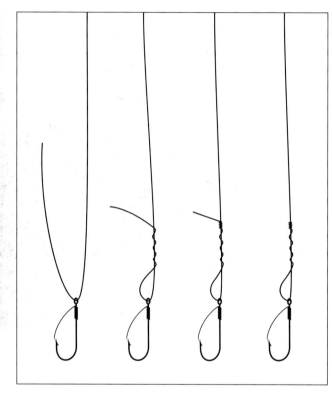

Single-strand wire makes a tough, low-visibility leader that's ideal for fishing for pike and muskie with light-weight lures such as soft plastic jerkbaits, or with topwater baits. Use a Haywire Twist to connect one end of the leader directly to the lure or hook, and the other end to a strong ball bearing swivel.

The easiest wire to use is single-strand, stainless steel wire, which is sold in many tackle shops. For most freshwater fishing, the 16- to 20-pound type is fine. Simply use a Haywire Twist to attach a small, subtle steel snap to one end of the leader, then attach a fine ball bearing swivel to the other. The Haywire Twist is easy to tie in the boat—just poke about six inches of line through the snap or swivel, bend it back around to form a little loop, and then twist the tag end around the main wire about five times. Then, make another four or five very close, tight wraps, trim off the tag end, and you're done. It's easy.

Rather than clip off the tag end, I simply grip it with pliers and flex it back and forth several times till it breaks. This gives a neater appearance and isn't as likely to foul weeds or get caught in the net. If you want to be very neat, dispense with the snap and permanently attach the leader to the lure's front eye. If you want to remove it, side cutters will snip it free.

Single-strand leaders made this way are very strong, tough for fish to spot, and light enough that they don't sink flies or affect the action of lightweight lures such as soft plastic twitch baits. Try making one.

Muskie Home Ranges

Because they have often caught the same muskie from the same general location, fishermen have always suspected that muskellunge are homebodies.

Now scientists, using elaborate radioelement tracking equipment, have confirmed that, indeed, this is the case. What they've discovered is that muskie establish home territories in summer and winter. And while the two areas are different, once they're established, a muskie will return to them year after year.

Water temperature seems to play an important role. In spring, when the temperature hits about 60 degrees Fahrenheit, most muskie head for their summer homes around weedbeds and off rocky points and bars. Here they stay till early fall, when water temperatures drop back into the 60-degree range.

For much of the autumn cooling down period, when water temperatures drift between about 60 and 45 degrees, the muskies' territorial instincts disintegrate, and they wander throughout the lake. But as soon as temperatures permanently drop below the 45-degree mark, the fish make a beeline for their winter homes.

When you raise a muskie, you can often return to the same spot later and find the fish again. Although it may not have hit the first time, it may be more active when you return.

The size of a muskie's home range depends on several factors. But the most important seems to be the size and depth of the lake where it lives. Home ranges may be as small as 15 to 25 acres, or as large as 50 acres or more. In virtually every case though, the biggest muskie has the biggest home range.

These scientific results confirm what many top fishermen have long suspected. If you catch a muskie, often you can return to the same spot a few days later and raise the very same fish. As long as we carefully release them, there will always be muskie for us to catch. But if we abuse this knowledge, we'll all be the poorer.

Pike Myths

Few people will argue that fishing has its share of old wives' tales, but the one that never seems to die is the one about pike losing their teeth in the summer. This, of course, is supposed to explain why some folks have a hard time catching pike in the warmer months of the year.

Look at it this way. In spring, when large numbers of spawning pike invade the shallows to spawn, catching them is easy. They're readily available, concentrated into obvious spots in big numbers, and aggressive as can be. Fishing's a cinch.

It's a different story a few weeks later when it gets hot out. Those shallows warm beyond the pike's comfort level, and the big fish beat it for cooler, deeper water. Yet anglers who continue fishing the shallows catch ... nothing. The obvious answer? They can't be feeding anymore...um...because they're losing their teeth! Yeah! That's it!

Not exactly. Pike don't lose their teeth at all. In fact, researchers have proven time and again that, in cool waters, pike grow fastest during the hot summer months when, according to the old wives' tales, they're not supposed to be feeding. Instead of fasting during these conditions, most northern pike are feasting. They're just doing it down deep, where many anglers never bother to look for them. Just because they can be caught in the shallows in spring and fall doesn't mean they'll be there when the water warms to a sticky 70 degrees Fahrenheit. No way. Pike—and big pike in particular—like cool water. In fact, they're more like lake trout than any other fish.

Justin and Wayne Izumi don't believe those old myths about pike losing their teeth in the summer. Instead, they fish a bit deeper and have a ball catching chunky northerns regardless of the weather.

So, when the weather turns hot, instead of grumbling about their losing their teeth, I fish for pike in deep water. In fact, some of the best northern pike fishing I've had during the middle of the summer has been in areas very close to, if not in, fairly deep water. This even applies to remote northern lakes where the summer is so short you'd expect pike to remain shallow year-round. Not so.

I can remember a midsummer trip and a late-season trip to Knee Lake in northern Manitoba, where we caught some very large pike by looking for isolated weed patches off of the bays in deeper water (10 to 15 feet). We found an abundance of large pike that had basically dropped out of these bays and stayed fairly close to their spawning areas but were around cabbage weed patches. One trip, Bob Paterson, director of marketing services of Mercury Marine, and I enjoyed some great pike action fishing a deep weed flat.

Interestingly, a few days earlier one of the young fellows in our group had caught a very large pike—in the 20-pound class—that had a unique scar. While Bob and I were taping a show segment together, drifting over the same flat, lo and behold, we caught the same pike with the same scar on it. It certainly goes to show you that catch and release does work as well.

And by the way, this pike, like all the others, had a full set of teeth.

Search Baits/Finding Fish with Lures

• Tip 96

As the old saying goes, if you can't find them, you're certainly not going to catch them. This is certainly the case with successful fishing. You have to find the fish first before you can catch them.

For many years now, what I try to do is cover a lot of water using a search bait. A search bait can be a crankbait, minnowbait, topwater lure, spinnerbait, buzzbait, inline spinner, vibrating crankbait—anything that you cast out and work horizontally through the water. What I do is work these types of baits and cover large expanses of water, trying to figure out (a) where the fish are, and (b) if they're active.

Many times, using these search baits, I find the fish don't even have to be all that active for them to show themselves. For instance, you could choose to work a large weed flat, eight feet deep with three or four feet of weeds off the bottom, in four acres of water. Chances are, if you pick apart this weed bed, you could be there the whole day, but if you use a spinnerbait and fan cast randomly over the weedbed, you can cover it more quickly. While videotaping for muskies on the Upper Niagara River with my guide, Mark Counsell, this past fall, we landed a couple of small muskies and had a couple of other follows, but for the most part it turned into quite a slow day of fishing. I was almost ready to throw in the towel when my cameraman suggested we go back to the area where we'd raised and caught a couple of fish earlier.

I agreed with him, although I was getting kind of hungry. After casting jerkbaits for seven hours straight, a man's got to eat, and we didn't have any food on board. After talking me into it, we tried one more pass. We went down this break line throwing jerkbaits and Mark shouted that there was a fish underneath his jerkbait, a great big Lindy Big M. I scrambled to grab another rod with more of a vertical type lure. I found one with a one-ounce Strike King Denny Brauer Pro Model Jig, and lobbed out a short cast. Unfortunately that jig was on a rod I didn't think I'd have to use that day. It was rigged from a previous trip. I'd forgotten there might be a problem with the line, the result of a previous backlash.

Regardless, I looked over at the Humminbird and noticed it was 21 feet deep and we were on a big drop-off. As we were slowly drifting in the current of the Niagara River, I finally pulled enough line off the tangled reel (it was a minor bird's nest), when, all of a sudden, my line went limp. I felt a little tick and as I lifted, it felt like I was hung up, then all of a sudden it started to thump a bit, and I was hooked to a 25-pound muskie.

As I'm fighting this fat Niagara muskie, I get it up to the surface right in front of the boat, then it goes off to the port side of the boat and it's only a few feet off the bow, then it swings over to the starboard side of the boat and I work it around so it doesn't hang up in the electric motor. I was saying to myself that now we can just put the cradle under it, and we have a great segment for the TV show. Just as we were sliding the cradle into the water, I looked back to make sure the cameraman was positioned and shooting, and gave the muskie the slightest dip of slack. It opened its mouth and the jig just fell out.

Obviously I felt disappointed at losing the fish, but the moral of the story? Had the fish never followed Mark's Lindy Big M, I wouldn't have hooked it. That's precisely what I mean about using lures to find fish. Even if you subsequently use another bait or technique to hook them, search lures often allow you to find fish.

This happens all the time when fishing with surface lures such as buzzbaits, or perhaps a Moss Boss surface spoon. When fishing in heavy cover areas, it's not unusual to have bass or pike blow up on these baits—boiling at them, but for reasons only the fish know, not becoming solidly hooked. You can follow up with a plastic worm or a jig and pig and catch the fish. But the fact is you found them courtesy of your original search bait.

If I'm fishing a new lake, I'll almost always begin fishing a spot by using some sort of search lure. Depending on the depth, the weather, and the species I'm trying to catch, I'll fish from the surface down to the bottom, but always using something that works horizontally, so I can cover water. If I catch fish, then I know they're in that location and they're hungry. If I get a little action, at least I know they're there. And if I don't get any response, I have also learned something—they're either not home, or they're just too inactive to chase those types of lures. That's my cue to try something slower. If I still don't get any hits, it's time to move on to spot number two. This is exactly the approach my brother Wayne and I have used to win dozens of tournaments over the past 20 years. It works.

CHAPTER 8

Walleye Tips

Jig Fishing

Tip 97

I probably use jigs more than any other lure because you can fish them fast or slow, swim them, pop them, drag them, you name it. They're versatile and come in many sizes and styles.

There's no doubt jigs are the number one artificial lure for walleye. People use grubs, tubes, shad bodies, and worms in every possible color. And most of them work very well. Jigs are great walleye lures because they work on the bottom where walleye spend most of their time, and because they so effectively mimic the walleye's natural foods—small fish, crayfish, and leeches.

Jigs consist of jig heads and bodies. Let's look at jig heads first. Jig heads are measured in weight, normally in various fractions of an ounce, such as ½ ounce, ¼ ounce, and ⅛ ounce. The most widely used range of sizes for walleye fishing are from ¹⁄₁₆ to ⅝ ounce—quite a range of weights.

The basic rule of thumb for jigs is to use lightweight heads in shallow water, then move to progressively heavier jigs in deeper water. Craig Ritchie has interviewed many of the best jig fishermen in the world. He uses what he calls the seven-foot rule, which means you should increase jig weight with about every seven feet of water depth. According to this rule of thumb, in water of seven feet or less, you'll usually have the best results with a ¹⁄₁₆-ounce or ⅛-ounce jig. From 7 to 14 feet (give or take) you'll usually want to move up to a ⅛-ounce to ¼-ounce jig. When fishing from 14 to 21 feet, you'll usually find a ¼-ounce to ⅜-ounce head works best. Once you pass the 21-foot mark, you'll want heavier jigs in the ⅜-ounce to ½-ounce size just to maintain any sort of feel. Approach 30 feet, and the stretch in even the best monofilament fishing lines becomes even more apparent. The answer is to once again increase weight.

When you consider that most walleye fishing takes place in water less than 40 feet deep, it's easy to see that jigs from 1/16-ounce to 3/8-ounce, or maybe 5/8-ounce, are the most useful.

The seven-foot rule is intended to give you a good starting point for fishing in calm, snag-free water. But this rule is flexible to allow for things such as current, weeds, and wind. For instance, add a bit of current to your pet fishing spot and you'll have a harder time getting down to the bottom. If you fish in currents, you may find the above weight guidelines useless. Depending on the current strength, you may need to start with 1/4-ounce jigs for fishing shallow water, and progress to heavy 3/4-ounce or larger models for fishing deeper water. The key, however, is still to increase size with every seven feet of depth.

The deeper you fish, the heavier a jig you'll need.

The same goes for fishing in windy weather, when your line gets blown into big bows and sensitivity goes down the tubes. Trying to cast and control light jigs in a stiff breeze is almost impossible, especially if you have to make long casts. You may need to begin with heavier heads than you would use normally. But increasing weight for every seven feet of depth still applies.

As far as head shape goes, most anglers find that the standard ball head works well. Wedge-shaped jig heads, which have the line tie right at the very front, work a little better when fishing in weeds. These tend to glide through the weeds more smoothly than a ball head, and there's less chance of the line getting caught on a stem.

Propeller jigs, such as the Lindy-Little Joe Lil' Hummer, add flash, vibration, and noise. They're great when you want a jig to sink a little more slowly, because the propeller adds drag.

As far as jig dressings go, grubs are still probably the hands-down favorite for walleye, particularly grubs in the three-inch range. Tubes are also great walleye baits, when rigged on the appropriate heads. Shad bodies are also popular.

One of the beautiful things about soft plastic bodies is that you can select one from a huge range of sizes and colors, and change it instantly. It's important to realize that the size of the body will affect how slowly or how quickly the jig sinks. Two identical jig heads, both 1/8 ounce, will sink at different rates if one has a huge, fat, four-inch grub and the other a thin, two-inch dressing. This is something to bear in mind when fish definitely want a slower or faster action than normal. Walleye in cold water can be reluctant to chase faster moving presentations, so slowing down can pay dividends.

The old-fashioned bucktail jigs still have their fans, and they can be deadly for walleye in weeds. They stay put when you get snagged in the weeds, unlike plastic grub bodies, which tend to get twisted out of place as you rip the jig free from the cover. Rip jigging, which is a great way to catch weed walleye, involves snapping heavy bucktail jigs hard through the vegetation, literally tearing a path through the weeds. You can't do it as well with plastic bodies because they slip down the hook bend and ball up, killing the jig's action. Bucktails are perfect for this, however, and have a great action when you work them this way. An option is to use a drop of one of the super glues that are available to hold the soft plastic on the collar of the jig and prevent it from sliding down.

Marabou jigs, which are tied using the soft underfeathers of a turkey, are also making a big comeback, particularly among tournament anglers looking for something different. Marabou was at one time very popular as a jig dressing, but it fell out of fashion in the late '70s and early '80s with the soaring popularity of soft plastic grubs. Yet marabou has an incredible action that's unlike anything else. That's why it's once again finding favor with top anglers on both the professional bass and walleye circuits.

When fishing with jigs, especially over the rocky bottoms that walleye love, it's important periodically to check your hook point. It's easy to bend or break off the tip of the hook point when bouncing your jig over granite. It could cost you a fish if you don't check now and then. Always take a moment to inspect the hook point after every catch, and after each time you get snagged. Every now and then touch it up with a pocket hook hone. Fishing jigs through the weeds and around rocks can also do a number on your line. Check your line regularly for abrasions. Many fish stories originate from break-offs that resulted from not retying often enough. You know, the good, old tale of "the one that got away because the line broke!"

Slow Steady Retrieve for Night Walleye

Tip 98

Walleye are superbly adapted to feeding in low light conditions and even in the dark of night. The unique membranes in a walleye's eye give them exceptional night vision—they use this ability to see in the dark to their advantage, feeding most heavily when they know they can see better than their prey. This fact explains why some of the very best walleye fishing happens at night.

Fishing for walleye at night is a little different from fishing for them during the day. You have to adapt your location, your presentation, and your lures.

I prefer to troll when walleye are spread out, or if I'm not sure where the concentrations are. Trolling lets me cover water to find fish more efficiently than by casting.

Trolling works especially well when you fish off long weedlines, beaches, straight shorelines, or river channels—spots where the fish could be here, over there, or anywhere in between. One great night spot is a shallow flat that adjoins deeper water. Walleye sometimes pack onto these flats after dark in pursuit of spawning bait fish. If it's a big flat, trolling is the only way to cover enough water.

Although a transom-mount electric motor will work for walleye trolling, I prefer a bow-mount, hand-controlled electric for better boat control. Boats are like ropes—they're easier to pull than to push. The bow moves through the water more efficiently than the flat stern end, using up less battery power.

You will probably have to make some turns here and there as you follow the weeds, which is where being able to control your boat's progress comes in. With the bow-mount electric, I just point the boat where I want to go and don't have to worry about currents or winds pushing me off course. If it's choppy I'll switch over to a gas outboard for power when trolling.

I caught one of my biggest walleye ever by trolling at night along a shallow weed edge. I had been taping a segment that involved casting Wally Divers and big Rebel minnows along a weed edge, and had caught several big fish up to about nine pounds from one location. We had shot enough tape at this location, so we decided to move to a different spot and shoot another segment. The new spot wasn't far away, and I didn't want to fire up the big motor for the short run, so I fired a long cast behind the boat and began trolling through some open water on another weedline while talking on my cell phone with Mike Melnik, who does the syndicating for our radio and TV series.

While I'm on the phone with Mike, and while the cameraman is getting set up with a new tape, I suddenly get a hit. At first I wasn't thinking about taping the fish, but then it began pulling line out. The drag was peeling off quickly even though I was using a medium-action baitcast outfit with 12-pound Super Silver Thread line. I told Mike I'd call him back, and we decided to roll some more videotape. Once the fish was near the boat, I could see it was huge! It turned out to weigh a hair over 13½ pounds!

The key with trolling, though, is to go slowly. Trolling as slowly as possible turns curious walleye into biters. The electric motor's ability to inch along at a snail's pace, without making any noise at all, makes it ideal for walleye fishing—especially at night, when fish will often suspend just under the surface or move into very shallow water.

It's no different when casting. Slow is the key.

I've done many trips where we cleaned up on walleye by fishing crankbaits such as the Cordell Wally Diver, Smithwick Deep Diving Rogues, and Rebel Spoonbills very slowly in the dark. The key was always an ultraslow, steady retrieve. Although walleye have excellent night vision, you still want to make it easy for them to find the bait. Erratic retrieves can fool walleye, while fast retrieves make it tougher for them to locate your lure. Stop-and-go retrieves are probably not as effective at night because, when you stop the retrieve, the fish might have a hard time figuring out where the bait is.

Night fishing for walleyes ranks at the top of my list for catching trophy walleyes.

Steelhead Tactics for Walleye

• Tip 99

They don't look alike, but spring walleye and spring steelhead have a lot in common. They both like current. They both like cool water and overcast skies. And they both respond to much the same fishing techniques.

Walleye sitting in current areas, such as below waterfalls and power dams, behave very much like steelhead, and respond to the same basic approaches and fishing techniques. Like steelhead, they can quickly become conditioned to fishing pressure. When everyone throws jigs, it doesn't take the fish long to figure out that eating jigs isn't a sensible thing to do—especially when other walleye that do just that are not seen again.

Fishing for walleye with steelhead gear often can trick even the most reluctant fish for the simple reason that almost nobody does it. Your approach is so fresh and different from anything the walleye have seen before, they practically fall all over themselves to get at your bait.

Best of all, nothing lends itself to fishing for walleye in current areas quite like steelhead tackle. Steelhead gear allows you to present a live bait in the most natural, effective manner possible.

Steelhead gear also allows you to fish with fairly light line in even strong currents, which is always a plus. Lighter line allows a more natural presentation, and is tougher for the fish to see, meaning you'll get more hits. The additional leverage provided by a long, whippy steelhead rod allows you to exert tremendous pressure on a hooked fish without fear of breaking it off, making this type of rod extremely effective for fighting fish in heavy currents. The long rod

Are they fishing for steelhead or walleye? At times it can be tough to tell, because when walleye hold in current areas, the same tackle and techniques will work for both.

153

also helps you to cover water by steering your bait around in-stream rocks and obstructions. The ability of a 10- or 12-foot rod to pick up slack line in a hurry makes it possible to deliver crushing hook sets when fishing in eddies and whirlpools, places where you might have trouble setting the hook with a shorter rod.

In the spring, you'll usually find walleye in current areas with their noses buried in the gravel. They're bottom-oriented, and both your gear and approach should be also.

For fishing on relatively snag-free bottoms consisting of potato gravel, sand, marl, and sheet rock, the simplest rig—a couple of suitably sized split shot about two feet up the line from your hook—works best. The walleye angler's cardinal rule—the simpler, the better—also applies when using steelhead gear. The best approach is the one with the fewest complications.

Cast upstream of the area you expect to hold the fish, and allow your bait to drift through it, flowing with the current. Once the bait is almost directly downstream from you, haul it out and cast again. This drift-with-the-current approach looks more natural than anything else to a spooky walleye.

You'll need to experiment to determine exactly how much weight you need to fish a given spot. Too much and your bait will anchor in one position instead of drifting naturally with the current. Too little and you won't get deep enough to interest the fish. The idea is to keep a reasonably tight line as your bait drifts downstream, and to be able to feel the sinkers continually tapping bottom. Of course, if you move to a new spot, you'll have to check once again to ensure you have the correct amount of weight.

Drifting a live bait on bottom using this sort of basic bottom-fishing approach catches walleye, but it also catches sticks and weeds. When fishing over bottoms with a lot of such cover, you might want to modify your basic rig by using a floating jig head instead of the hook, to add a bit of color and to make the bait more visible to the fish.

In off-colored water, you can steal another trick from the steelheaders and add a short piece of colored yarn to help attract attention. Simply tie an inch-long chunk of yarn right into your knot, or loop it in place using a snell. It might look a bit ridiculous having a gaudy chunk of fluorescent pink yarn at the head of your worm or leech, but this technique works. At times you can even catch walleye just on the yarn itself, which is a big plus when fishing in spots where you have a lot of bait-stealing panfish.

When you drift fish for walleye in a current and get hung up on the bottom, it's usually the sinker that gets caught—not the hook. Steelheaders almost always fish over such snaggy terrain, and have devised a number of intriguing ways to deal with snags.

The simplest way to deal with snags is to rig up with a three-way swivel. Tie your main line to one eye of the swivel, then add a 6- to 12-inch dropper line to eyelet number two. To the third eye, tie a four-foot monofilament leader and your hook. The weight goes on the end of the dropper line.

The advantage of this rig is that when your weights get caught on the bottom, a smooth, steady pull will strip them off the end of the dropper line, so that you don't lose the whole works. Simply replace the weights and you're back in business.

Especially brutal bottoms may require that you get off them entirely and rig up with a float. Standard steelhead models are just about ideal for most walleye fishing, and work quite well. So next spring when those walleye are tough, think steelhead.

Walleye and Light

Tip 100

Light levels affect the location and activity of all game fish, but no species more than Canada's ever-popular walleye. Most folks don't realize it, but the eyes of a walleye are very specifically adapted to enable it to see and feed best in low light conditions.

So, if you want to consistently catch numbers of walleye or bag a trophy or two, you've got to consider light levels. For instance, if you're fishing a super-clear walleye lake and the sun's beating down, you should probably start fishing in at least 20 to 30 feet of water, where the light barely penetrates. Most likely, that's where you'll find the walleye, hanging out where the sun is less intense. Remember, they don't have eyelids, sunglasses, or hats. When the sun shines brightly, walleye have to find shade or go deep to where the glare's easier to take.

In lakes that don't have any deep water, look for walleye in dense cover such as a thick bed of cabbage or a big patch of coontail weeds. It's here that the walleye can burrow and hide from the light.

In addition, a dark or stained walleye lake would make a better daytime choice than one that is crystal clear. In fact, the darker and dingier the water, the more the walleye like it.

Another way we beat adverse light conditions is by fishing in the early morning and late in the evening. These are prime times to catch walleye because, during these periods, few of the sun's rays penetrate the surface of the water. Conditions like this are ideal for walleye either

Trophy walleye in clear lakes represent one of the toughest challenges in fishing. Try heading out early or late, or on overcast days, when light penetration is reduced.

155

to move shallow or to come out from cover to feed. Or try fishing at night, when these fish often feed the heaviest. On lakes with very clear water, night fishing can be the only time to consistently catch bigger fish. I can certainly tell you the vast majority of big walleye I've caught have been hooked in the dark. Clear, moonlit nights can still be surprisingly bright on the water, especially with a full moon. It's bright enough that you can see what you're doing, yet dim enough that walleye feel perfectly comfortable gorging themselves in the shallows. Besides, it's not too likely you'll see many other people out there fishing, or have any water-skiers zooming around to put the fish off. Keep quiet as you fish and you'll be amazed at the action.

Tip 101 · Weed Walleye

Over two decades of tournament fishing and producing a television fishing show, I've been lucky enough to travel to many places and to learn about different ways of fishing. No matter where you go, there always seems to be some local favorite way of doing things. I've also seen how easily anglers can fall into a rut, especially when they fish for a given species of fish in only one type of location or with only one technique.

This might be especially so in the case of walleye, since they're found over such a big chunk of North America. Just about everywhere you go, people associate rocky points, reefs, and shoals with walleye. It just goes to show how popular these fish really are.

It also goes to show just how many people ignore the weeds when looking for walleye. Yet weeds can offer some of the very best walleye fishing.

Weeds attract walleye for several reasons. First, the fertility means plenty of food, including smaller fish and leeches. Weeds provide cover and protection from predators, while also offering oxygen and shade. Shallow, nutrient-rich lakes are definitely walleye magnets.

Drop heavy jigs into openings, into inside turns, and along points in the weed growth for walleye that few anglers ever target.

The key to catching weed walleye is to find the best spots within the weeds, and to fish using techniques that give you the advantage. Most anglers have heard the term "weedline," which essentially means the line formed where the weedbed ends. That's your best starting point. Look for changes in the weedline, whether it be places where the type of weed changes (such as patches of cabbage weed mixed in with coontail or milfoil) or physical changes in shape, such as points, subtle turns, or corners. In many lakes, the weedlines can be untapped fishing areas.